Risk-Shaped Ministry

On Going out to the People of God

TERRY BIDDINGTON

Foreword by Una Kroll

RESOURCE PUBLICATIONS, INC.
San Jose, California
rpinet.com

Reprint Department
Resource Publications, Inc.
5369 Camden Ave, Suite #260
San Jose, CA 95124-5809
(408) 286-8505
(408) 287-8748 fax
editor@rpinet.com

Library of Congress Control Number: 2014948839

Printed in the United States of America

14 15 16 17 18 | 5 4 3 2 1

Design and production: Patty Sweet
Copyeditors: Barbara Mellen and Caroline Thomas
Front cover photo: Fiona Biddington

Dedication

To Una Kroll, who has given bread to so many.

Contents

Foreword

Terry is an Anglican priest, teacher, lecturer, and university chaplain who has experience of Christian ministry in a wide variety of multifaith, multicultural, institutional, and voluntary sector contexts. He has spent decades working with young people and is in a strong position to communicate what they are saying about their beliefs and aspirations.

He is also a prophet. A prophet's job is to look at where society is, to predict where it is going and to warn his generation when radical change is needed. In this book Terry suggests that "the urgent priority for the Church today is *not to get people inside and convert them* so much as to get outside and enable people, in the distinctiveness of their own unique personhood *to become whoever they are meant to be.*" This change of direction would mean that Christians might become a positive leaven in society "so that the *unconditional* nourishing and flourishing of *all people* is the normal and expected goal and desire of the church" (Introduction).

Terry's reappraisal of the priorities for "the church of the twenty first century" leap out from the text for me because I have been trying to live that way as a self-supporting minister of religion since 1970, taking strength from my Christian discipleship to get thrust in to the concerns and problems of people who have never been inside a church building.

Terry is one of the prophets I have met during my long life who have encouraged people like me to live a risk-shaped ministry. He is not, however, writing only for a group of

Christians who have already developed risk-shaped ministries. In his remarkable and seminal third chapter he invites all Christians to engage with their own communities to change attitudes and bring about the "going out into the world" that he considers so important. He urges his readers to re-imagine what might happen if we reconnect with secular society, and become re-enchanted with the potential in all human beings to bring about desirable social change.

But espousing a risk-shaped ministry is no easy task, especially when some church members seem set on retreating from the world into comforting zones of separatism. It contradicts a prevalent idea among some Christian communities that they would be "contaminated" by close contact with a secular society and should therefore avoid participation in its governance and activities.

Consequently, this is a tough book to read; but it springs from a deep belief in the ability of the Christian faith to bring about transformative change. Having lived a risk-shaped ministry for many years, I support Terry's ideas. I do not avoid people who do not come inside our church doors. I learn from them, and, together with them, I try to find ways to make a positive difference in society.

In this book he gives theological shape to our lives, and issues us challenges to reflect on the nature of risk-shaped ministries with a set of questions at the end of each chapter to promote group discussion. You cannot hurry through this book. If you use it as a workbook you will need to go slowly, argue with Terry and yourself, consider his propositions carefully, and use, or adapt, his suggestions in your own communities.

Una Kroll
September, 2013

Introduction

Christian Ministry Today

This book tries to sketch out a new take on Christian ministry for the twenty-first century: a time when humanity stands at a crossroads, both in our relationship to our planet and to the universe that is our home, and also in our desire—or not—to build an inclusive global human community.

It is a book that tries to begin from a new place because the world itself is very different now from what it was before, and because many people in our world have either turned their backs on traditional forms of belief, church, and religiosity, or else have retreated into more conservative and exclusive expressions of theological, religious, or cultural mindsets. It is also important to note, right from the start, that I'm convinced that the transformation of Christian communities and of the church will come from engagement with "the outside." That is assuredly where the Spirit of God is most active; and always has been. So this is a book that tries to urge those on "the inside" of church to listen hard and look carefully—with fresh eyes—and to take seriously what can be learned about ministry from those on the outside and at the margins.

Consequently, I try to ponder if a new matrix for transformative Christian ministry might be created and what it might look like. I wonder whether, and how, Christian communities might be encouraged to reach out—unconditionally—beyond their church buildings, and be transformed and enriched by their encounters "on the outside"; and whether, in turn, they might be enabled to create and share opportunities for *all* people and communities to encounter, dialogue, learn, and flourish.

This is, of course, risky stuff, so, by definition, what I am describing here is a *risk-shaped* ministry. In my *Risk-Shaped Discipleship* (2010), I explored how very "risk averse" western society has become, with risks having to be minimized at every opportunity, and where *risk-taking* has become almost synonymous with irresponsibility, if not criminality. At the same time this is even more true for the church, where the ever-declining number of attendees is outstripped only by the ever-increasing irrelevance with which its institutional structures and fossilized belief system are perceived.

This new reality has plunged the western church into "grief mode." The old ways of doing things are no longer working and it is still not apparent where the solution lies and what shape any future church might take. What is clear, however, is that, to many in the church, real risk-taking does not seem a particularly welcome or creative response to the situation in which it finds itself. Even so, we might hope that the church—unlike perhaps the finance sector—does, in fact, possess the capacity for self-transcendence—if it chooses to activate it.

While the church is—for better *and* for worse—a community of memory that not unsurprisingly needs to spend time attending to the just still-beating pulse of its former glories and work through the pain of its loss, *it should go without saying* in a community of resurrection that Jesus tells us, "Let the dead bury their own dead; but as for you, go and proclaim the kingdom of God" (Lk 9:60). The church needs to look honestly and creatively to the future. Today, as never before, Christian ministry is bound up with creative risk-taking; not only to overcome the numbness and resistance wrought by the historic decline and disintegration of the church, but as part and parcel of the proclamation of the kingdom-kindom of God at a time when, for so many people and communities, and for the planet itself, risk and consequence have never been for such high stakes.

So here is a book that tries to explore what creative risk looks like in a community of resurrection; who is called to enable risk; and what the consequences might be both for risk-taking and, indeed, for not responding to the call to risk all we have on the possibility of flourishing for our planet and its people.

The Back Story

A few years ago I read an article in the UK press entitled "A New Dawn: How Britain Became a Pagan Nation" (*The Guardian*, June 21, 2009). Its author, Cole Morton, suggests that "paganism is going mainstream … [and is our] new national faith," and that "we're all pagans now," a circumstance he attributes to a combination of things. He is greatly exaggerating the situation, of course, but there has indeed been a resurgence of interest in various forms of spirituality among certain groups. This resurgence, in the West generally, is largely among those in mid-life who have become disenchanted with the church over several decades. It manifests itself in a desire to explore less- or non-doctrinally based types of religion and popular, more experiential and non-hierarchical forms of spirituality; often grouped under the umbrella of "DIY religion" and "new age" spirituality. This resurgence has coincided with a renewed interest in, and concern for, environmental and ecological issues, and with the huge popularity of so-called "healthy living," "grow your own," and "self-sufficiency" lifestyle "choices" that often seek to make temples of our own bodies with our egos the gods within.

Alongside this is a phenomenon that sees the majority of young people looking to popular forms of culture and self-expression to provide the social, existential, and transcendent functions previously provided by religion and religious frames of reference, practice, and community. And not least, there is the appeal of global youth culture to satisfy the need for heroes and savior-figures, for an exploration of the possibility of magical or supra-human power, and for a sense of the experience of being caught up in the mystery of arcane mythologies, quests, enchantment, and adventures. It is clear, too, that young people are also desperate for a way to transcend the limitations and boundaries of earthly human existence and connect with and explore the mystery of the universe. And what wouldn't most of us give for a magic wand that really works, a friendly ghost, angel, or god to fight our battles and keep us safe, or for a credit card that pours out guaranteed cosmic blessings for all eternity!

This widespread desire for authentic experience—"aliveness"—and for the assurance of a secure place for us in the world—"at-homeness"—results from the sense that so many of us share of living in a world that is threatening to disintegrate around us. We say there is no certainty any more. We feel ill at ease and alienated and imagine life in the past to have been so much better. We allow ourselves to believe there are enemies lurking behind every bush and such countless dangers and perils waiting to beset us that we need to take flight from reality in consumerist or therapeutic routines to numb our psychological angst, or to distract ourselves from our deep needs and eternal hunger. Or else we try to protect ourselves with militaristic and technological "solutions" to mask our feelings of fear and insecurity in the world and the sense of our smallness before the mysterious vastness of a universe we know and understand so little and cannot control.

So Where in the World Is the Church?

Given this state of affairs we might be forgiven for thinking that our churches should be packed with people overcome with all manner of psychosomatic traumas and dysfunctions of the soul. And yes, some parts of the church are indeed bursting! Supremely those that try to offer intellectually certain faith, guaranteed eternal salvation, and—ideally—health, wealth, and happiness in the here-and-now, are seeing boom times. And we can see why.

But the success of this conservative section of the church also seems allied to the way in which the beliefs it proffers are rooted in, and reliant on, notions and practices that are predicated on the need to belittle and exclude those whose faith is *different and therefore surely less true* than theirs, in the vilification of those whose lifestyles are *different and therefore manifestly inferior* to theirs, and in the hostile suspicion of those who have *different and therefore invalid* attitudes, goals, and approaches to life and to its big questions and challenges.

Such an approach to church is rooted in the need to create scapegoats and enemies. It reduces religion and belief to the level of the sports field where only one team is best, only one side can win, and where to be second best, or worse still to lose, is simply *not* to count at all. Here there's an assumption that God and the Holy Spirit have to be "on our side" if we are ever to be able to *defeat* temptation, *vanquish* the scary world we live in, and *win* (and not simply *run*) "the race that is set before us" (Heb 12:1). For it is only in achieving this victory that we can "please" Jesus who, despite all the rhetoric, is *often treated* as though he were an eternally vigilant team coach or manager who brooks no failure: *not after all he went through for us!* This may sound something of an impious caricature, but it is what many people actually appear to believe, and it is certainly the tone of many sermons and homilies from this segment of the church!

Of course, the daily reality for the mainstream church in the West is that we are not at all overflowing with people. In fact churches across the UK and Europe are relatively empty most Sundays and holy days, and even in the United States, where church-going is a more common and socially acceptable activity, the popularity and influence of the church is in slow, long-term decline. While we may argue about the precise statistics, it is clear that the church today occupies a lesser place in the public arena and consciousness than it did fifty years ago.

People no longer flock to worship or to hear what the preacher has to tell them. Bibles gather dust, crosses and crucifixes have become largely just fashion items, confessionals are mostly disused, and clerical "wisdom" or advice is more or less universally ignored. People have voted with their feet and are doing their own thing—or not. So let's return to Cole Morton's suggestion and bring on the pagans, wiccans, bards, heathens, druids and, yes, the Jedi knights!

Learning from the Alternatives

Now I, for one, cannot despise or belittle these groups. I have met many and have been generally impressed by their open minds and hearts, their humanity, and their gentle respect for other people and for creation. I'd go further, in fact, and say that I can well understand why people have walked away from churches that have more than tended to discourage questions, alternative thinking, independent spiritual exploration, and a sense of dynamic connection with, and care for, the universe.

I recently held some seminars on prayer and spirituality with a humanist group. While the issue of "God" was, of course, divisive and irresolvable, I was impressed by the way in which daily routines of mindfulness and meditation (the term "prayer" had too great a religious cachet to be useful to them), and a real desire to develop appropriate, ethical, and integrated disciplines of "spirituality" were central to the lives of many group members, though the "S" word itself was contentious for some. Indeed, after we had explored the meanings of such practices, their content and usefulness, one group member suggested that, had such conversations happened at his church when he was a choirboy, he might still have been there today. Other members concurred.

These are not isolated incidences. In the UK, where the Church of England, as the "Established Church," takes responsibility for the great bulk of funerals of non-church attendees, and where infant baptism—though still a widespread practice—typically doesn't automatically suggest parental commitment to the Christian faith, it is remarkably common for a pastor or priest to have extraordinarily powerful encounters and conversations. For people everywhere are keen to discover a meaningful spirituality, explore practices of stillness and meditation, and reflect on issues of ethics and values, the nature of God, reality, and the visible presence of non-Christian faiths in the local community.

Finding a Christian Lifestyle

Indeed my own experience at such moments, as well as in my work with students and young people, suggests that if there is a single issue that arises time and again, it is the business of what it means to live a life that values embodied experience, promotes responsible ethical service and action, and that cherishes those special qualities, perceptions, and creativity that flow out of the self-consciousness of our human condition, fallible contingency, and inevitable mortality. In short, people seem to want to have a *lifestyle* that's meaningful, fulfilling, and satisfying.

Now it is undoubtedly true that this understanding of lifestyle largely reflects the influence of consumerism on our contemporary world. At a recent "Mind, Body, Spirit" fair I was struck by the number of different "lifestyles" on show and "for sale," and by how our own stall representing the churches was similarly viewed. One woman had brought her son along in order to "find a spiritual path for him." On approaching us she told him: "Let's see if this'll do" (Biddington, "Spirituality in the Market-place," in *The Way*, October 2007, 119). There was a real sense, too, that, if one lifestyle "didn't work," or didn't "live up to expectations," or was "too demanding," then it could be "ditched," or else "taken back and exchanged for another," because people had *bought it* just as they might buy any other item or service.

It is also true that those who feel they lack such a lifestyle are fascinated—and perhaps a little awestruck or afraid— of those people who do visibly display and celebrate their religious lifestyle and discipline. The fact that Sikh and Jewish men courageously sport distinctively *unfashionable* headgear, Hare Krishna devotees with painted foreheads wear strange robes and practice veganism, and Muslims are obliged to pray five times daily and abstain from alcohol, leaves many young people wondering *what a Christian lifestyle might look like*; what its uniquely distinguishing—and therefore also potentially appealing—characteristics might be. How it is recognizably different, given that, these days, the ubiquitous cross or a crucifix itself communicates little anymore about that distinctiveness. For whether we like it or not, Christianity is now popularly perceived to have little relevance or appeal for people today, and the Church is deeply associated with negative, life-denying, out-of-date, and irrelevant attitudes and practices; if not, indeed, with altogether darker things.

While "spiritual seekers" are very open to learning to meditate "Buddhist style," explore the world of Sufi practice, or sit at the feet of a Zen Master, there is little interest in discovering more about Christianity. The religious habits and spiritual disciplines of the Christian faith are *simply not recognized as being an attractive lifestyle option* for the majority of intelligent, compassionate, mature people, to say nothing of those who value being "cool" or having "street cred!"

Opening the Treasure Chests

It could yet be different. Despite the fact that, ironically, within the church itself, there is generally a very limited awareness of the range and value of its own spiritual treasures and insights, it is slowly waking up to the opportunities that are beckoning.

Considerable energy and money are being expended in the UK and elsewhere on an array of activities under the "fresh expressions" label, which sees churches involved in a wide range of initiatives. On the one hand, there are new forms of practical ministry and service such as distributing bottled water outside night clubs, cleaning deprived neighborhoods, and setting up community spaces where people might meet. On the other hand, there are new styles of collective worship such as "café church," where people sit informally around tables and enjoy coffee and cake while they discuss issues, receive Christian teaching, sing a song or two, or else take part in simple meditative styles of worship that eschew creeds and sermons. Alongside this are the well-known introductory courses such as Alpha, Emmaus, and Quaker Quest and, on TV, popular "docu-soaps" that feature people exploring the possibility of faith by spending time in Christian monasteries, on Muslim desert retreats, or—a few years ago on the Turkish TV station Kanal T—the challenge of being locked in a room with a rabbi, Orthodox priest, imam, and Buddhist monk to see which of the atheist contestants converts first. (The prize: an all-expenses-paid trip to the holiest shrine of their new religion!)

It is all creative, fascinating, and entertaining stuff. And, for the churches, it is also about getting people back into the church or in its mission-speak, "going for growth." But the big, and often unaddressed, question is whether it is even possible to bring the horse back through the stable door so long after it has bolted—to say nothing of what the horse might be fed with if it decides to stay!

So What's Inside?

Unfortunately, much of what "fresh expressions" is about is actually nothing more than a rather stale representation of classical theological formulae and traditional teaching: about the Trinity, the "saving work" of Jesus, the superiority of the Christian path, and the need to forsake the temptations of "the world, the flesh, and the devil." Those people who do venture over the threshold—just to see what's on offer—frequently discover that becoming a Christian seems to require little more than first, submission to a fairly constrained theological world view and to a well-worn, often clichéd understanding of "salvation history"; one that starts with the impulse to make amends for the sin of Adam and Eve—two people who actually never existed—and then demands the "acceptance of Jesus as Lord and Savior, turning to Christ, and following his way."

Second, people are all too often met with the anticipation that they conform to a particular historic cultural identity that still assumes white, male, heterosexuals are the "normal and best" shape, and so provide the pattern for all; and where everyone else—females, non-whites, gays and lesbians, the disabled, and so on—have to conform themselves by means of silent, painful contortions—if they wish to remain.

"Fresh expressions" presents Christianity as all about proselytizing, conversion, and church-going, rather than spiritual or ethical practice and engagement with the world.

It offers a view of the church that is all about membership, accepting a "package" of belief, and a risk-averse and world-denying spirituality. It does nothing very much to demonstrate or encourage God's love in action. It rarely, if ever, speaks of the kingdom-kindom of God.

Obviously, the church, like any other social group, needs its communal identity. But it is my contention that what is *meant to be* the distinctive identity and function of the group called "church" is *not to be* an ark for the elect and the redeemed, a watertight raft to keep us from drowning in life's stormy seas, a safe stronghold for unchanging doctrine, a holy huddle for the religious conservatives, or a club for life's "spiritual conformists." Such ideas may once have been common perceptions—indeed, cherished descriptions—but the evidence today is that such an approach is manifestly failing to appeal to the majority of people in the West. We need to think again. In particular, we need to take our lead from that extraordinary risk-taker, Jesus of Nazareth.

Changing Priorities

The starting point of this book is that the urgent priority for the church today is *not to get people inside and convert them* so much as to get outside and enable people, in the distinctiveness of their own unique personhood, *to become whoever they are meant to be*, to make the best they possibly can of the one life they have, and to contribute—as far as they are able—to the ongoing transformation of their communities and of the world. And that, in turn, will require some hard thinking about the nature of the church's ministry.

The task for followers of Jesus today is to reverse the direction of our historic assumptions about what the church is for and to reconnect with our neighbors without any assumptions or conditions about the nature of their response. The task is to properly become the leaven of which Jesus spoke, the leaven that enables the dough to take whatever shape it will, and to become the best bread it can be, *so that the unconditional nourishing and flourishing of all people* is the normal and expected goal and desire of the church and its members.

The problem, of course, is that the declining congregations in so many places are very often *unable* to do this. It is not that they are necessarily unwilling. As the part-time pastor of a small suburban church a few years ago, it was clear to me that the elderly congregation was very keen indeed to step outside the church. What prevented them was the lack of human capital—people, time, and energy—to go beyond the effort required to maintain their internal congregational life, and to step beyond the church doors to the extent, and in the ways, that were necessary for effective outreach and growth.

So perhaps the task I'm proposing is indeed too much for some congregations. Perhaps, too, it can only be achieved by those groups who are released from the need to maintain particular high-maintenance forms of congregational life: buildings, clergy-led liturgies, hierarchical denominational structures, (though this seems singularly unlikely to happen; at least until such time as the currently-constituted churches do finally collapse). Perhaps the task I describe is, therefore, restricted to those congregations who have been enabled to experience an energizing connection between the radically inclusive values of the gospel, and the empowerment that flows from a genuine desire to fundamentally open their hearts and minds to those values, so as to engage creatively and fearlessly with the calling to be companions on the way with those who have no express interest or desire ever to step inside the church.

For this calling, once discerned and actualized, has the effect of largely dissolving the distinction between the church and the world. In this new way of looking at things, as we will see, the locus for perceiving God's activity is not the church alone, but also the world outside it. Identifying this calling also questions the disabling, and structurally and financially problematic distinction between lay and ordained ministry on the one hand; since the "stuff" of the sacraments to be blessed is no longer exclusively the bread and wine on the altar, but the lives of all people, and the world and creation as a whole. On the other hand it serves to highlight, once again, that it is *all Christians*, by virtue of our calling and baptism, who are called to be priests and pastors of, and in, this world-affirming vision and risk-filled ministry.

But no sooner do these words appear on the page in front of us, than we are surely struck by their tremendous implications.

A New Understanding of Leadership

Now, I am not wishing to anticipate the end of the church—it seems to be doing that nicely by itself!—but I do think we are overdue some really creative step change about the nature and purpose of ministerial leadership. For leadership is something I think the church has got itself into a bit of a muddle about.

On the one hand we want our leaders to be inspirational, but on the other, we also seem to want them to be safe and "media-friendly," so desperate are we to avoid upsetting people. And there seems to be something of an obsession in the church with identifying "leadership qualities," so that vast amounts of money and resources are spent on training people to be the *right sort* of leader. Then, ironically, all too often we refuse to let them lead!

While much of this is well intended, of course, I'm convinced that it is also deeply misguided; not least in its association of leadership with a solely priestly and ordained function. It is a real tragedy that priesthood and priests—"hieros" in Greek—have lent their name to the authoritarian power relations associated with ecclesiastical *hierarchy* rather than the ethics of servanthood as modelled by Jesus. Too much of the focus, as the church shrinks, is on the leadership and ministry of priests, when priestly leadership in the church is simply one gift among many, and priests are no more important in God's purposes—or in the church's transformation—than are lay followers. While, of course, ordained leaders do have a specific and crucial role, it is not, as we so often assume, to "do all the ministry" and simply *be helped* by the laity with the things for which the clergy don't have time. Rather, as Hans Rudi Weber puts it, "The laity are not helpers of the clergy so that the clergy can do their job… but the clergy are helpers of the whole people of God, so that the laity can be the church" (Diocese of Bath and Wells website, 2013).

What the church needs is not better leaders, but better followers—followers, not of the clergy, but of Jesus Christ. What the church needs for its transformation is a flowering of different forms of discipleship and a flourishing of the gifts of all of God's people, known and unknown.

Ordained clergy exist to enable the priestly ministry of all believers and the recognition and practice of the ministerial vocation of all people in response to today's global, multi-cultural, secular world. And from where I stand, "global, multi-cultural, and secular" are the exciting hallmarks of a flourishing and radically inclusive future for the human community and for the practice of Christian ministry. I believe passionately that there is a desperate need for the Christian church to rediscover its vocation, and a real role for it to play—alongside the other world faith communities—in leading the effort to birth a fuller, more responsible, and more inclusive humanity. I owe it to my children—and believe we all owe it to all children everywhere—to ask hard questions about what the shape and nature of ministry are for those who dare to call themselves Christian disciples in this generation. For I believe there is a really creative Christian vision for the future to be rediscovered: a lifestyle and a ministry for all those who choose to identify with, or respect, the way of Jesus. It is out there waiting for us. It is a *risky* world, a *risk-filled* lifestyle—and, so, a *risk-shaped* ministry.

A Risk-Shaped Ministry

Risks are part and parcel of life. A willingness to engage with risk is what holds together—*just*—the fabric of our existence: the warp of our experience and the weft of the meanings we find there. We do all understand the idea of risk—albeit perhaps reluctantly—though often we rail against it, pray to be protected from it, insure ourselves against it, and work hard to minimize or avoid it. And we create or long for past, present, and future utopias where all risk has been eliminated: a garden in Eden, the heavenly new Jerusalem, and, for many people, the church itself where we can be all safe and snug inside! "Please don't preach the gospel next time you come," a church elder once told me. "It disturbs the congregation." Yet Christian ministry is properly and necessarily all about engaging with risk and with being disturbed by what Walter Brueggemann aptly calls "the threat of life" (*The Threat of Life*, 1996, *passim*).

The Christian faith, as traditionally understood, has been, in one important sense, all about risking everything for the future: Jesus' death on the cross, his future return, the "eschaton" at the world's end, the "Day of Judgment," the after-life, and all that *endless* eternity. But now, at this point in our history, I believe we are called to use that "openness to the future,"—"*ad venturam*" in Latin—to discover how Christianity is *meant to be* all about the "adventure" of living out our lives in the here and now: in the pain of human contingency and mortality, as much as in the joy and delight of celebrating the new life that is ever coming to birth all around us.

But there can be no adventure without some degree of risk. Our Scriptures are full of people setting out into the future and following an intuition, an instinct, or a sense of calling; stepping into the unknown and running serious risks because they understood God to be asking that of them. Abraham, Sarah, and Moses walked into the scorching wilderness; Jeremiah and the prophets stood up against the authorities and elites of their day; Jesus followed a hunch and consented to a possibility at his baptism. And even Peter, Paul, and the other disciples eventually said "yes" to God's call.

Are such deeds just "stories in the Bible"—or are they more than that? Are such risks just for *other people*—the acclaimed "heroes" of our faith—or do we *all* share the same calling in our own day?

And So to This Book

My aim is to explore some of this risk-shaped thinking about ministry in today's world. The overarching principle is that the Christian communities that make up the church need to get out a great deal more and engage with the people in the local community, with their neighbors "on the block"; with those who rarely, if ever, attend; and among those who have little, if any, interest in the church.

The object of this exercise is, for those of us who call ourselves disciples of Jesus, to engage *unconditionally* with those in our communities. There must be no deliberate intention to proclaim the gospel, convert people, or to bring them inside; though people always remain at liberty to attend. The object is to listen and learn, intentionally, from those "outside" about what they think is important in life. There will be many interesting interactions along the way; times when it is okay for us to share some of our stories. But what may more likely happen is that we discover that we are *enabling each other*—Christians and non-Christians together—to discern, celebrate, and live out creative responses to life's challenges and opportunities.

It is very possible that not many people will want to follow us back into church. But that's not the point. What is highly probable, however, is that friendships will be made, tales shared, and yarns stretched across our communities so as to forge new networks of relationships. Times of celebration and feasting will follow and—with luck, and a good draught from the Spirit/spirit abroad in the world—a regenerative space will open up in the midst of us all. There will be a space for *re-imagining* how things could be, for *reconnecting* people in an inclusive and life-affirming community, and for working together to create a place of *re-connection* and *re-enchantment* where the mystery, awe, and beauty of everyday life can be experienced and celebrated anew. It will be a space for taking up the challenges of a creative risk-shaped ministry and for seeing where they lead us.

In Chapter One: "A 'Tea and Biscuits' Theology," we take a hard look at the church as it has been, and where it might be being called in the future. We look at how theology has tended to exclude and marginalize people, to the point where ordinary folk—whether or not they are church-goers—have been effectively robbed of language to articulate their own religious and spiritual experience. We see how a false spirituality has evolved within the church that actively prevents individuals from flourishing and communities from thriving, and how clericalism has stunted the idea of vocation and ministry. In short, we'll explore why we need a new kind of church, a new understanding of vocation, and so begin to sketch out what it will take to encourage the flourishing of a new kind of ministry.

In the following chapter, "Taking Time Out," we'll do just that. We'll leave the church one night after worship is over and step outside to experience the darkness. Christians go on endlessly about being "people of the light," and about "overcoming the darkness." But God creates the dark too, and we need to be people who know how to explore all that the darkness holds, and the treasures it promises. We need to cross over, out of the light of certainty, knowledge, and security, and learn how to *unlearn* in the darkness. How to thrive with doubts, let go the need for a consoling voice amidst the silence, and learn how to listen, see, and serve again. In particular, such a church—resurrected in the darkness—will need to rediscover, reclaim, and offer a rich ministry of spiritual encouragement, discernment, and affirmation of the deep longings of all people, regardless of whether or not they follow the way of Jesus. Such a *more excellent ministry* (to paraphrase Paul) may just offer the church the possibilities for its radical transformation into the kind of therapeutic community that may more fully realize its true vocation.

Chapter Three is entitled "Relearning the 'Three R's': Re-Imagining, Reconnecting, and Re-Enchanting." It is about looking again at how the church might discern the Spirit amid the contemporary chaos of the western world. It looks at how the fascinating business of spiritual meaning-making, and of seeking a "God of one's own," offers opportunities for an amazing practical ministry of reconnecting with people, serving the community, and empowering people to explore their authentic humanity and the meanings and names they give to their experience of being alive. We will also look more deeply at how the human imagination has become a most suspect and neglected accessory in our theological tool kit, but one that is key to risk-shaped ministry. We will see how the enchantment we long for is already there in our communities, in our innate ability to wonder, and in our drive to creativity.

This leads naturally enough to a chapter called "Be Friending," which attempts to explore what "radical friendship" means, and how we might overcome ambivalence towards "otherness" and begin to create communities of resurrection. There building radical friendships leads to a discovery of true human potential that might then allow the divine to be birthed in our midst, and of how allowing ourselves to rediscover the experience of being guests amongst strangers might reveal the contours of a "greater personhood" to share with the world.

In Chapter Five: "Celebrate!," we explore what it really means to give thanks and celebrate, and whether Jesus' ministry might offer clues to help us imagine ways to improve our capacity for experiencing what it means to be blessed and to live truly fruitful lives of witness. This will lead us into an exploration of the nature of worship and whether this might be re-imagined through a new lens. Might worship, for instance, become a means of discovering ways of being "at home" in the "wildness" of God? Does this, in turn, lead to a doorway through which we can experience radical amazement, "shalom," playful joy, and a way of nurturing— and being nurtured by—the ever re-creative presence of God in the universe and in our local communities?

The final chapter, "Risk-Shaped Ministry," begins by exploring what it means to give birth to creativity. Here I want to place the idea of discovering, naming, and celebrating creativity right at the heart of ministry to, and among, individuals and communities. I want to show how encountering creative newness, welcoming it all around us, and giving ourselves permission to be co-creators with God, are central to the transformation that our world needs right now. This is perhaps the real sacramentalism that the church is called to practice, perform, and proclaim: to become an instrument by which the global human family is encouraged and enabled to imagine life as it never was, and then to imagine that newness and fullness of life into being

But Will Everyone Say Amen?

I am enormously grateful to David Ackerman, Hugh-Rayment-Pickard, Jayne Prestwood, John Walker, Marc Ciufo Green, Peter Sutton, and Stephen Canning for their generous conversations, detailed observations, and incisive comments on the text. Above all, I have a profound gratitude to Una Kroll both for writing the Foreword and for many years of friendship, godly conversation, and often tough questioning. If any name deserves to be associated with the title of prophet, it is rightly hers. And it is to Una that I warmly dedicate this book.

Time to explore!

Here are some ideas for you to discuss with friends, Christians, or church leaders in your local church or community:

- What do you feel about the society you're living in? What, if anything, would you wish to change about it? Do you agree that the world is a scary place, full of hidden dangers? How might you respond to the mystery of the universe?

- What do you think of the idea that some religious groups see themselves as superior to others? What is your understanding of the value of the other world faiths? Is it possible that God loves them equally?

- How would you reply if someone asked what you think being Christian is all about? Is there a non-negotiable essence to Christian identity and lifestyle? What is it that excites you about your own faith?

- What is more important: having people convert to your faith or enabling people to become who they are most truly meant to be? Have you ever been attracted to elements of another faith, and, if so, what were they?

- What do you think of the idea that faith is an adventure that involves inevitable risk? Is religion truer to itself by keeping people faithful to revealed truths from the past, or by equipping them with the resources to face up creatively to the challenges of the present and future?

- What do you think is the real task of the church in the world? Do you believe the church has a future?

- What are your thoughts and feelings at this stage about the shape of this book, and about the journey that I'm proposing for us to travel? What do you think is God's calling for you? Are you up for an adventure?

CHAPTER 1

A "Tea and Biscuits" Theology: The Church and Its Vocation

Part 1: A "Tea and Biscuits" Theology

Like a Mighty Tortoise

There's a famous, but anonymous, version of the hymn "Onward, Christian soldiers" that has the line: "Like a mighty tortoise; moves the church of God. Brothers, we are treading where we've always trod."

This idea has become widely used to parody the church, implying that the church moves forward incredibly slowly. The analogy reminds us that, until recently, the venerable giant tortoise of the Galapagos Islands was heading slowly, if inextricably, towards extinction. That is, until careful and determined nurture began to provide it with a slim, but realistic, chance of long-term survival. This in turn begs the question of whether similar attentive nurture would assure a future for the church, and what this nurture might be.

The church has been around for over two thousand years, and it is easy enough for many of us to assume that it hasn't changed at all. But that's not the case, for the church's evolution is, in fact, clearly visible to anyone who cares to look at how it has adapted over time to different cultural environments. The Orthodox Church in Russia, the Coptic Church in Egypt, the Pentecostal Church in Brazil, the Roman Catholic Church in Africa, and the Anglican Church in Scotland are all very different creations. Indeed, many believers from across the world would almost certainly fail to recognize, for example, the worship of the Coptic Church as being even Christian, given that the ritual prostration in prayer at its heart has become entirely associated with Islam; yet it adheres to probably the earliest form of Christian worship to be found anywhere.

This slow evolution of the church has taken centuries. And it has been a highly contextualized process, combining largely unconscious adaptation with occasions of conscious change—like the establishment of the Church of England in the sixteenth century and the second Vatican Council in the 1960s—mingled, inevitably, with times of active resistance to change.

The church has also played many roles in the different cultural contexts in which it has found itself. During the early Roman period it was very much outside the social structures and often despised by virtue of its inclusion of women, slaves, and those perceived as social inferiors and outcasts. During the Middle Ages the church was at the cutting edge of knowledge, closely aligned to the powerful social elites, and the sole provider of healthcare and poor relief. However, since the eighteenth century Enlightenment in the West, the church has increasingly been regarded as the home of intellectual and social conservatism and the bastion of stubborn moral intransigence and reactionism. In the nineteenth century, and with the rise of liberal democracy and capitalism, the western church began to lose much of its role in the provision of social care and education; while across the twentieth century, with its awful global conflicts, continuing social liberalization, and rapid technological developments, the mainstream churches have found themselves hemorrhaging significantly from their membership and struggling to manage their finances and historic buildings. Finally, the late twentieth century saw the global rise of aggressive fundamentalist forms of belief and witnessed their impact on the more established expressions of the mainstream church.

Consequently, at the start of the twenty-first century, questions about the church's future, direction, and function—its ministry—have never had more poignancy. Is it moribund and fated for extinction? If it did disappear, would anyone *actually lament* its passing—or would it in fact be a great relief to us all? On the other hand, we might ask what kind of careful nurture might work to coax it back to life. And if it is to survive, what might its role be? In short: What would, could, and should the church look and feel like if it were, after all, to turn an evolutionary corner and step confidently into the challenges of the future?

Taking the Temperature

For a considerable time now Christian scholars, practitioners, and ordinary church members, deeply concerned for the communication of the gospel and the survival of the Christian way of life, have been urgently drawing our attention to the challenges we face.

In the USA, the biblical scholar and preacher Walter Brueggemann has highlighted how, within both society and the church, "the dominant culture is … resistant to genuine newness and real surprise" (Brueggemann, *The Message of the Psalms*, 1984, 22). In Britain, writer Alex Wright talks about the church's vocabulary being "hopelessly out of phase with that of the people and lives to which its message is directed" (Wright, *Why Bother with Theology?* 2002, 8), while theologian Sally McFague characterizes the church's teaching as full of "tired clichés" (McFague, *Speaking in Parables*, 1975, 22-26, *passim*). Another British theologian, Mary C. Grey, speaks of the "stagnation" of the churches (Grey, *Sacred Longings*, 2003, 80), while the American evangelical teacher Miguel De La Torre suggests that the church "has … become an ornate prison" (De La Torre, *A Lily among the Thorns*, 2007, 84). In the UK, environmental theologian Anne Primavesi sketches out the church's complicity in what might be called a "theology of death" (Primavesi, *Sacred Gaia*, 2000, 95), while radical theologian Don Cupitt makes the breathtaking comment that "religion is a serious threat to human well-being" (Cupitt, *Above Us Only Sky*, 2008, vii), and that "anyone who remains serious about religion needs to break with organized religion" (70).

Plastic Faith

Christian belief has become inflexible, fixed, and increasingly fossilized, as the church has used both the Bible and its theological discourse to maintain the boundaries of its own identity and whatever privilege, social standing, and influence it has, or aspires to. This narrowing of vision has been described, perhaps most succinctly of all, by English Catholic theologian James Alison as the outcome of our "being trapped in too small an identity" (Alison, *Faith beyond Resentment*, 2001 and 2006, 201).

This idea that the church has allowed the Christian faith to become *too small* resonates with very many people. Christianity is fundamentally all about Jesus and the belief that faith is experienced and articulated in relation to him. This remains true whether we talk about having a "direct relationship with the living Jesus," or whether we prefer to see that relationship mediated and expressed through the sacraments and prayer, or by our engagement with the Scriptures.

What happens over and over, however, is that faith begins with this dynamic relationship, but ends by morphing into a static belief or an inflexible doctrinal system whose truth is to be asserted *over* or *against* all other religions, faiths, or philosophies. This is true historically, as the first disciples' lived experience of Jesus was handed on to others in the form of oral memories and subversive stories which were gradually—if inevitably—incorporated into edited collections of Christian Scripture and codified into the doctrines, dogmas, and creeds of the church. And it is also true for us, whenever we readily slip into preferring to reify or objectivize our faith—to encapsulate it in ready-made statements of belief—rather than working to keep faith dynamic, living, and *open to fresh insights and new understandings* as we reflect upon the experiences and meanings of our unfolding adventure of faith.

We seem to prefer keeping Jesus safely bound in Scripture, securely enclosed within a well-edited translation, and comprehensively limited by our traditional interpretations— "the polite hermeneutic of the Church" (Brueggemann, *The Message of the Psalms*, 1984, 16)—rather than commit ourselves to *working at the relationship* and to *being open to the radically unexpected* promptings of the Spirit. We have sought to reduce God, and belief in God, to the bare functional data that we can store on our plastic credit ("creed-it?") card of faith: wonderfully small, highly manageable, and conveniently available in our pocket or purse, whenever the need arises for urgent miraculous activity or instant divine intervention.

And this is all so dreadfully *unbiblical!*

Decent or Indecent Faith?

Argentinean liberation theologian Marcella Althaus-Reid argues that, at the hands of the church, a "pornographic network of theology" has been developed to marginalize people–individuals and groups—who fail to fit into its carefully constructed and self-serving categories of righteousness, holiness, and acceptability (Althaus-Reid, *From Feminist Theology to Indecent Theology*, 2004, 98). She says that "… theology has literally been putting people out on the pavements of the church for centuries" (74), that the church is a "theological industry … creating needs and selling [the] goods of salvation" (112), and that "… churches are vast enterprises where capital is accumulated and invested for profit" (133). All pretty damning stuff!

At the heart of her argument is the idea that the church has quite simply ignored the voice of ordinary people and their experience, and deliberately prevented theological debate and fresh thinking, that the body of theological discourse, doctrine, and dogma so cherished by the church is, in reality, one that has been constructed by educated white males, and serves simply to maintain the "decency and order" of a self-serving status quo and, further, that those people who fall outside this narrow social group must be "encouraged" to see this privileged belief system as, quite literally, the will of God, with no possible alternative to be countenanced. Accordingly she suggests that, if this situation is ever to be challenged and critiqued, theology needs to become *indecent.*

While Althaus-Reid is speaking predominantly of the situation in Latin America, where the church has been accused of complicity with the ruling elites at the expense of the landless poor and marginalized, there is a very real sense that, more generally, the church could be said to have indeed tended to use theology to exclude and marginalize people: to the point where ordinary folk—whether or not they are church-goers—have been effectively robbed of language to articulate and explore their own religious and spiritual experiences or existential concerns.

Second-Rate Provender

For far too long the church has been promoting and offering what might, in the West at least, be called a "tea and biscuits" theology. That the theology on offer has become the equivalent of the rather poor provender traditionally shared at church after Sunday worship: those basic dry rations, cheap to provide, frequently rather weak, tasteless, stale, and generally entirely uninviting, that go by the name of "refreshment."

Furthermore, it is clear that this kind of attitude has, in turn, allowed an easy contentment or accommodation with all that is second rate to evolve within the church: a false spirituality that actively prevents individuals from flourishing and communities from thriving.

This provision of poor provender and inauthentic spirituality is made manifest in the desire to control, correct, manage, police, or else interpret people's experience for them. It is a mechanism that denies people the right to explore for themselves the richness of their own experience by offering them "orthodox" language and an "approved" conceptual framework for understanding and making sense of their lives. Over time this has created a culture of dependence that tends, rather unhelpfully, to infantilize people and further prevent them from engaging with these issues for themselves. So we have "Mother Church," who likes to keep all her members "children." Additionally, as we have seen earlier, the language and concepts that the church uses to go about this task have become unbelievable, fusty, clichéd, incomprehensible, and largely empty of meaning for most ordinary people. Of course, people can all too often be intellectually lazy and lack curiosity, not least we church folk. And for too long, and all too readily, we have been happy to be spoon-fed or to live off pre-packaged rations. But it is killing us!

The time has come for us to abandon the sleek publicity and marketing strategies proposed by recent church initiatives—such as the UK's "mission-shaped church" drive—that seek only to increase numbers of worshippers and church groups and, instead, to re-examine our faith and live out our discipleship precisely by taking up the call to create a risk-shaped ministry of unconditional service and action in the world. For Christian discipleship is meant to be about living the core teachings of Jesus, active commitment to the world and its people, a dedicated exploration of the "priesthood" of all the baptized, and a willingness to be and to make a difference: to build the "kingdom-kindom" of God here on earth and not merely to attempt to fill churches.

Consequently, we need to find ways of reconnecting with people in a language that is meaningful and which enables them—and us—to articulate our individual and collective experience of the ever-contemporary aliveness of the Spirit of the living God and of the radically inclusive vision of the Jesus of the gospels. We need urgently to step outside the church-shaped box in which we have been content to remain, in the hope that others might just come along to join with us on the outside. We must shake off the easy and familiar habits and practices that have built up around us over the centuries and let our faith speak in and through our unconditional love and gratuitous practical care *for* the world and in the belief that we have so very much to learn *from* the world.

On Stepping outside the Box

The New Testament has several extraordinary accounts of people doing just this. While they are stories that will be recognizable to most church-goers, their familiarity usually rests upon particular well-tried interpretations of the events.

So, in the story of "The Syrophoenician Woman's Faith" (Mk 7:24-30; see also Mt. 15:21-28 where she is called "Canaanite"), the traditional focus is upon the actions of a woman who begs Jesus to heal her daughter of her "demon possession." She cleverly counters Jesus' initial rebuttal: "Let the children be fed first, for it is not fair to take the children's food and throw it to the dogs" (7:27), with her quick-witted, "Sir, even the dogs under the table eat the children's crumbs" (7:28), and so receives her desired outcome. Her daughter is healed. Similarly in John 4:4-42 we find the story of "the woman at the well." Here Jesus encounters a woman drawing water outside the Samaritan city of Sychar. The traditional interpretation focuses on their extended dialogue and on Jesus' knowledge of her past life—"He told me everything I have ever done" (4:39)—that enables her to return to her community a different woman.

Both stories are generally understood to be about women who find healing and restoration at the hands of Jesus. This interpretation continues to have meaning for the Christian community. But this reading ignores something of equal, if not greater significance, than the easy transaction between savior and saved that fulfills and reinforces our accepted beliefs and expectations about Jesus and about ourselves. For both stories have a regularly *unexplored* dimension that shows the two women (their identity reduced to those unnamed racial stereotypes: "Syrophoenician" and "Samaritan") engaging confidently with Jesus and challenging his own thinking. In both encounters, the women oblige Jesus to confront the boundaries of his own experience, and what might even be said to be his own prejudice. For the women are foreigners, so outside the Jewish community, one a Gentile, the other a Samaritan. But they are also *women*: and to orthodox Jewish thinking, they are none of his concern!

Jesus refers to the "Syrophoenician" woman and her people as "dogs." This is a phrase that has frequently been played down in Bible commentaries, with suggestions that such language was "rare," or that Jesus actually uses a "playful" diminutive form of the word such as "puppies" or "house pets"; and that he is teasing her! But would Jesus joke with the woman at such a time of obvious distress for her? Would Jesus contradict his previous character and actions in this way? Or might we instead consider the possibility that this incident shows Jesus as a man of his time; a man with human limitations; a man who had grown up within a certain set of negative cultural and religious assumptions about "outsiders"? But as a man who is—nonetheless—being called to step outside those same limitations.

Likewise, in the story of the "woman at the well," it has become all too easy to focus on the supposed sinful life of the woman with "five husbands, and the one you have now is not your husband" (Jn 4:18). But why does no one ever consider the possibility that she has finally rebelled and chosen to step outside a religious system that obliges her again and again to become the wife of a previous dead husband's brother? (See Mk 12:18-23.)

The long conversation between Jesus and the woman operates around the tensions between Jew and Samaritan. We read "he *had to go* through Samaria" (Jn 4:4, my emphasis), that "he came to a Samaritan city" (5), that "a Samaritan woman came to draw water" (7), and that "the Samaritan woman said to him, 'How is it that you, a Jew, ask a drink of me, a woman of Samaria?' (Jews do not share things in common with Samaritans.)" (9). The conversation is certainly somewhat flirtatious, with the Greek phrase "sharing things in common" able to refer to drinking vessels, conversation, or sexual activity. But the extended references to "our ancestors" (12 and 20) and "you worship what you do not know" (22) and "true worshippers" (23) maintain a focus on the difference between the two communities and on being restricted by the expected protocols for social interaction with foreigners and with women.

When the disciples return with food they are, indeed, astonished enough that Jesus is speaking with a woman. But when the woman returns to the city and the disciples try to persuade Jesus to eat, his response is extraordinary:

Jesus said to them, "My food is to do the will of him who sent me and to complete his work. Do you not say, 'Four months more, then comes the harvest'? But I tell you, look around you, and see how the fields are ripe for harvesting" (4:34-35).

We can almost see Jesus' mental horizons being stretched. From a belief that his mission was only to his own people, the "house of Israel," he appears to have had something of a conversion experience as this random encounter opens up for him the discovery that the expected harvest is all around them, even in Samaria. His worldview has suddenly expanded with new possibility and new direction. And, as a result, he spends two days in a place he had originally only grudgingly chosen to pass through out of necessity.

Peter's Experience

A similar "threshold experience" is recounted in the story of Peter and the centurion Cornelius (Acts 10:1—11:18). Cornelius, although a Gentile, was a "god-fearing man" (10:2). He had sympathies with the Jewish faith, though had not chosen to convert. He prayed in his own way and tried to lead a devout life. And one day he has a vision and is told by an angel to send for Peter. The following day Peter prays before the noon meal. His hunger intrudes upon his prayer, as it will, and he, too, has a vision:

> He saw the heaven opened and something like a large sheet coming down, being lowered to the ground by its four corners. In it were all kinds of four-footed creatures and reptiles and birds of the air. Then he heard a voice saying, "Get up, Peter; kill and eat." But Peter said, "By no means, Lord; for I have never eaten anything that is profane or unclean" (10:11-14).

As a practicing Jew, Peter's response is entirely understandable. (When he later recounts the vision to the other Jewish disciples in Jerusalem, his more extensive list "I saw four-footed animals, beasts of prey, reptiles, and birds of the air" [11:6], suggests the way the total visceral disgust and nausea he feels had continued to play upon his mind.) So the heavenly voice speaks again to Peter, and challenges this revulsion: "What God has made clean, you must not call profane" (10:15). But it takes three attempts to soothe his loathing before he is able to consider calmly the meaning of what he has seen.

As he is struggling with the implications, the men sent by Cornelius arrive, (three men, the same as the number who went down to Sodom [Gen 18], and who went up to sacrifice Isaac [Gen 22], suggesting that the hand of God is at work here too). Peter returns with them. When he arrives, Cornelius immediately falls at Peter's feet and begins to "worship" him: as any good centurion of the Italian cohort might naturally be inclined to do when petitioning an authority figure or someone considered socially superior. Perhaps Cornelius' confused behavior is a response to the fear and awe he felt during his earlier angelic visitation. And Peter, too, is evidently thrown by the presence of so many others, presumably a mixed Jewish and Gentile audience, assembled there to witness what might happen.

To this end, Peter begins by addressing the "religious irregularity" of the gathering itself, perhaps to show his own legal observance, but perhaps, too, to deflect any criticism of his own presence there: "'You yourselves know that it is unlawful for a Jew to associate with or to visit a Gentile; but God has shown me that I should not call anyone profane or unclean'" (Acts 10:28).

As Peter speaks to the assembly, he amplifies what he has discovered from struggling with his own recent vision:

"'I truly understand that God shows no partiality, but in every nation anyone who fears him and does what is right is acceptable to him'" (34-35). Although he has hitherto held that God's revelation was to the chosen people of Israel alone, Peter has come to understand "'that everyone who believes in him receives forgiveness of sins through his name'" (43). And while Peter is speaking these very words, the Holy Spirit comes upon everyone in the room. It is an extraordinary moment of unexpected revelation:

> The circumcised believers who had come with Peter were astounded that the gift of the Holy Spirit had been poured out even on the Gentiles, for they heard them speaking in tongues and extolling God (45-46).

The radical amazement of the moment, enacted in the baptism of those present that day, is short-lived. For Peter has to face the other disciples back in Jerusalem: "the circumcised believers criticized him, saying, 'Why did you go to uncircumcised men and eat with them?'" (11:2-3). And so Peter is obliged to tell the whole story again.

By now, however, he has distilled the visceral emotion of both his own vision and of the astonishing events in Caesarea into a reasoned argument:

> "The Spirit told me to go with them and not to make a distinction between them and us" (12).

> "And as I began to speak, the Holy Spirit fell upon them just as it had upon us at the beginning" (15).

> "If then God gave them the same gift that he gave us when we believed in the Lord Jesus Christ, who was I that I could hinder God?" (17).

The criticism is silenced and all the disciples begin to praise God for giving "even to the Gentiles the repentance that leads to life" (18). The hitherto accepted interpretations of the foundational experiences of those *Jewish* disciples are torn up and discarded. What has happened is utterly unexpected. And they stand agape as an entirely new world, with its attendant risks and challenges, beckons them forward into an unknown future.

A New Release of Energy

This extraordinary story describes the moment and the process by which the historic course of the development of the Way, as Christianity was originally called, was changed forever. As John O'Shea has observed, Peter's original understanding of God, and the ways of God, had "completely imprisoned him" (O'Shea *Gospel Light*, 1998, 149) and the release was utterly dramatic. But for Peter and those first disciples, the full significance of this event could not be foreseen. The manner in which the Jewish Jerusalem-based church was, relatively soon, to become marginalized within the broader gentile Christian world was completely outside their purview. But just as Jesus did, *they took the risk nonetheless!* They heard and discerned God's prompting and, though the outcomes—for themselves and for their community—were very far from clear, they said "yes." *As a direct result*, an undreamt of, exponential, world-changing surge of energy was released. And people throughout the then-known world were able to catch a glimpse, a sight, a sound, a scent, a perception of a new vision for human living and a new recipe for human flourishing.

Surprise, Surprise!

The narratives we've been considering are of immense significance. To suggest that Jesus experienced radical amazement and had aspects of his inherited belief system pulled, like a rug, from under his feet, is a thought not to be considered lightly. Nor is the exploration of how Peter and those first Jewish disciples had their worldview turned upside down something to be undertaken without the deepest respect for their religious inheritance.

What is more remarkable still—even than the historic significance and impact of these amazing threshold experiences—is that the catalyst for these events, the means whereby God had apparently chosen to work in this matter, are not the great heroes, the revered, the saintly or prophetic figures, or the "anointed leaders": Moses, Peter, or even Jesus. Rather, it is those ordinary folk—the unnamed women and the foreign soldier—who stand outside the community, outside the chosen, outside the fold, outside the appropriate socio-economic categories, outside the list of "regular attendees," whom God chooses to change the shape and direction of the future. It is a desperate woman with a sick child. It is a woman wounded by the religious system and by the hypocritical expectations of "decent and polite" society. It is a man struggling to explore his own spiritual experience and trying to lead a worthwhile life. *These are the ones who open up the future.*

I Said, "Outside the Box!"

It is no longer just a question, if it ever was, of the church and its members having the "Christian" good will, kindness, generosity, humility, godliness, righteousness, compassion, or selflessness to engage with "those in need": with the marginalized, the outcasts, the abandoned, the destitute, the unworthy, and the poor. It is no longer sufficient to justify our existence—to say nothing of our desire to maintain our buildings, infrastructures, internal hierarchies, and privileged status—by thinking that the church alone is God's agent in the world, or that the future will be bright if only everyone joined with us.

The time has come to recognize that the future flourishing of the Body of Christ is bound up with those who do not, and perhaps will never, choose to attend church and belong as we have done. The time has come to acknowledge—painfully—that the church of the future may likely not be one that we might readily or easily recognize.

Perhaps all we can do is to acknowledge the pain and explore the feelings we share with Peter and those first Jewish Christians, feelings of a wistful, tender, regret—and perhaps some anger—for the passing of something we have taken for granted and cherished; something that has given meaning to the particular expression of our lives. Then, again like them, we can dare to rise above those feelings and say "yes" to the real and exciting possibility of becoming a creative and necessary part of a new vision, and of the next stage of God's evolving relationship with humanity and with the world.

Time to explore!

Here are some ideas for you to discuss with friends in your local church or community:

- Someone once defined prejudice as all the "common sense" we learned from our parents. What prejudice have you experienced as a Christian? And in what prejudice might you be complicit as a church-goer?

- How would you describe the ways in which your church, faith, and religious practice create a "box" which you inhabit? Is this a good place to be; or are there times when you feel the box is getting too small or tight for you?

- How do the stories of Jesus with the two women and Peter's vision speak to you? What have been your own experiences of radical discovery and amazement?

Time for some action!

Here are some suggestions for you to try out:

- Alone or with friends, go to worship in a church of a different tradition from yours. Be as adventurous as you can! Make a point of introducing yourself and saying why you are there. What do you experience? What are the similarities with and differences from your own church?

- Meet with some non-church-going friends. Ask their opinion of the church, why they don't attend, and what they think about the Christian faith. Don't attempt to defend your views or correct theirs; simply listen and make mental notes. Then share your discoveries with your congregation.

- Take some time as a congregation or small group to look at the kinds of outreach, mission, or social engagement the various churches offer in your local area. Visit some of them. What is their purpose? Is it to serve, to evangelize, to draw in, or something else? How do they relate to the maintenance and support of a local church? Or are they offered gratuitously to the community, with no strings attached?

For church leaders:

- What percentage of your time is spent on maintenance tasks; and what on outward- facing activities? Is this the balance that you would wish?

- What are the good and less good things about the church and congregation in which you offer leadership? What things cause problems? Where are the points of resistance to change?

- What things would you want to change about your church and congregation? Why?

- How might you be preventing change or new developments from happening in your congregation?

- How could you discern and address this possibility?

Part 2: The Church and Its Vocation

Towards a Fresh Start

At the heart of the problem with much of what passes for purposeful activity within the church—the way it conceives of and articulates its proclamation, theology, ministry, and mission—is an obsession with "apologetics." That is to say we limit our communication largely to (usually embarrassingly clichéd) explanations of "what it is Christians believe." We are forever clarifying to "non-believers" those concepts we consider to be central to the Christian faith: the incarnation, atonement, and bodily resurrection of Jesus; the divinity of Christ; and so on. But all too frequently we forget the bigger picture. We have, to echo James Alison, *too small a vision.* We act as though "belief"—and believing the *right* things—is more important than anything else about our ministry, discipleship, and Christian lifestyle. And perhaps, too, we fall into the trap of assuming that "believing the right things" is just as important to everyone else.

But even if it were, in fact, correct that belief is so important, then we need to be aware that many of the best discussions about belief—and some of the very best theology—happen outside the church. It happens often in the unlikeliest of places and as a result of impromptu creative encounters with those who are neither Christian nor, indeed, believers of any kind—and we're generally missing out on all this!

The truth of this is hinted at in the gospels' presentation of Jesus' own way of operating. For his entire vocation, once he had consented to it at his baptism and explored it during his struggle in the wilderness (Mt 4:1-11; see also Lk 4:1-13), was *not to promote or explain* Jewish belief, but to restore to the community those whom the Law excluded. Neither did he seek to bring them physically back into the synagogue or to make them regular temple attendees. Most of those whom Jesus encountered would, by virtue of their on-going occupations or bodily imperfections, be forever regarded as ritually impure and so continue to be excluded from the "sacred precincts."

Jesus' ministry was, rather, to *extend* the category of ritual "cleanness" to cover, affirm, and include those who had previously been called "unclean" and excluded. Thus those who had been "non-persons" under the Law were enabled to experience, in their own bodies and as persons within their communities, the wholeness, flourishing, and "shalom" of God's "kingdom-kindom."

Jesus' concern was with the whole ethical edifice of the Law, which operated by means of a power dynamic that dominated and discriminated against people. This system excluded people and denied them the chance to engage in the rituals and practices that gave them access to what we might call "meaning-making": the chance to have a fulfilling religious and spiritual life and a sense of place and belonging within the community for which God had created and called them.

Finding a New Sense of Vocation

There was a time when the idea of vocation—of calling—had a deep resonance with people everywhere. God was understood to have created the world; but the Hebrew verb *"barah"* of Gen 1:1 means both to "create," and to "actualize." So in creating us, God is directing us in the ways which will actualize our potential. It is as though, at our creation, God speaks to us and calls us into particular forms of potential and promise that are unique both to our species and to each of us in our own individual humanity and personhood. And everything has been created, called, and actualized. Everyone, quite literally, has a calling, a vocation.

Jesus, too, has a vivid sense of his own unique vocation, discerned powerfully at his baptism when, rising out of the water, he hears a heavenly voice calling to him: "'You are my Son, the beloved; with you I am well pleased'" (Mk 1:11; Lk 3:22; see also Mt 3:17). This sense of divine vocation to his own birthright and destiny as a "Son of God" is one that he seeks to extend to all those he meets on his journeys. For all are called to join the community of those who are being re-created—and re-called—to a life of healing, service, and inclusive belonging. The astonishing creativity of those among whom this discovery was made—that original gospel band of followers around Jesus, as much as in the early church community described in Acts—was as transformative as it was infectious.

Unfortunately, given the hierarchical societies in which early Christianity existed, it was impossible for the church to maintain for long the radical notion that *all people* might be called, empowered, and transformed in this way. So the notion of having a vocation eventually became restricted to an entirely male order of *ordained* deacons and presbyters who swiftly took control of the church and its practices and who served to maintain and police its boundaries.

Since then, save for the very recent usage of the term to denote a specific range of "vocational" training courses (often for less well-paid kinds of employment), the idea of vocation has become almost entirely bound up with the notion of clericalism. To this extent a more meaningfully creative, inclusive, and collaborative sense of the vocation of all people—*believers and non-believers alike*—has been effectively lost.

Yes, we might justifiably rail about the dominance of the clergy that so often actively discourages lay participation. And we could easily lament the way in which overwork and unrealistic expectations put unbearable pressure on the fewer clergy that are coming forward and for which the church can afford to pay. And we should certainly recognize that clergy have often become the scapegoats for the sorry state in which the church finds itself. But the significant issue, to my mind, is that we need to discover and share a new and *alluring* sense of inclusive vocation.

The Nature of Vocation

Just as vocation originally referred to God's creation of the universe, by creating, speaking, and calling it into being, so vocation is intimately connected with matter, atoms, and stardust; with the stuff of life—with flesh, bodies, and bodily fluids. Any Christian understanding of vocation must by necessity also include this dimension.

Christians need to be people who are familiar and at ease with the embodied nature of vocation, for vocation is not a calling to the mind or spirit alone. Vocation does not seek to separate the immaterial heavenly soul from its supposedly sinful earthly body, as people once believed. So a fresh understanding of vocation, of God's calling of individuals and communities, must help us to engage and celebrate the very physicality of our once-so-despised bodies and senses, at least as much as we have hitherto chosen to rely, more or less exclusively, on our minds and spirits for moral discernment, social action, and imaginative, creative discipleship and ministry.

Consequently, in a world where we have gradually allowed market forces to hijack "very successfully the language of desire and longing" (Grey, *Sacred Longings*, 2003, 193), and have lost the word "erotic" almost entirely to pornographers, a new sense of vocation will enable us to articulate and engage with what Mary Grey goes on to call the "new economies of desire" (203).

For desire—from the Latin "*de sidere*" meaning "from the stars"—has become the currency of the world in which we live. It is desire that, for good or ill, lies at the heart of what it means to be human and to be community. We desire because we lack and are incomplete. We desire because we are afraid. We desire the "Other" that lies beyond us. We desire to be part of the greater whole: the families, communities, and nations of which we are a part. We desire because we want to be known and loved. We desire because we are motivated. We desire because we are called further into the future, the unknown, and the mystery of God. We are creatures of desire: "I am, I want and I will," observes Ann Morisy (*Bothered and Bewildered*, 2009, 10).

So a significant vocation for the church lies in becoming fluent in understanding the language of desire; for desire may call us on or hold us back, distract us from our course or inspire us to continue. Desire may give rise to selfishness or urge us on to build communities of justice, equality, and radical amazement. We must use the *visceral knowledge*, given us by virtue of our embodied vocation, to foster an ability to discern and navigate the ubiquitous dynamics of desire that affect us all, and which can—if we choose it—be put powerfully at the service of others and for the building up of humanity.

A Fresh Appreciation of Personhood

This new understanding of vocation will, in turn, sketch out a fresh valuing of the *diversity of personhood*. For, if all matter is called into being, then all people are called into their own unique, inalienable personhood; into personal "meaning-making"; and into creative relationship with others. All people, without exception!

For too long the church has behaved as if only a certain class of people (white, educated males) was divinely designated as more valuable to God's purposes than others. But more critically, in its concern to prioritize and protect this one group, the church has disempowered and disabled all the others. It has done this by infantilizing them, cultivating a culture of submission and obedience, and by actively denigrating and discriminating against them. Anyone who is not normatively white, educated, and male becomes a "problem": women, the mental and physically ill and disabled, those deemed socially unacceptable, gays, lesbians, transgender people, and those who can be otherwise readily categorized as "perverse" or "defective," or else simply as "not-like-us." In the eyes of many church-goers and leaders, these are effectively non-persons who can be routinely singled out for direct and indirect discrimination. Anyone who doubts this should look at those churches that have negotiated exemption from legal anti-discriminatory laws. And yet these very individuals and groups are largely the same people with whom Jesus had most to do!

For far too long we have clung to the idea that personhood—being a "real" person—equates with some idealized state of physical perfection, rational ability, and normative gender, sexuality, and race. What Genesis 1 reminds us is that God calls creation "good," and not perfect. And what a renewed sense of vocation helps us to appreciate is the fact that personhood is a generous and inclusive "rainbow" category that cannot be reduced to a single preferential color, religion, gender, sexuality, and physical or mental ideal.

Accordingly, a clear assertion that every individual is a unique person, and that *personhood*—in all its God-given diversity—should be the simple and irreducible benchmark by which we recognize and value a brother or a sister, becomes the means whereby people of faith can make creative connections with others. Many of them are already further down this road of inclusive thinking than we are.

An inclusive model of personhood, that doesn't judge people if they fail to measure up to traits that are deemed normative by the narrow measure of statistical averages and historical and cultural prejudice, is one that most readily fits both with the vision of the kingdom-kindom acted out by Jesus, and with the sense of God's vocation—calling—of all people. For, irrespective of the particular accidents and characteristics with which people are born, or which emerge as a result of their upbringing or social or cultural situation, *it is clear that God calls all people into maturity and wholeness.* God wishes that all people, everywhere, should flourish and find justice and fulfillment, and Christian ministry needs to address itself more to that divine mandate than it has hitherto managed.

A New Take on Spirituality

A new sense of the richness and diversity of persons, and of God's calling all people to fullness of life, inevitably results in *myriad different expressions* of what it means to live a spiritual life.

So, it is sadly ironic that Jesus' notion that "'I came that they may have life, and have it abundantly'" (Jn 10:10) has manifestly failed to be adopted as an unconditional and non-negotiable undertaking within the life and ministry of the church. Far too often what passes for fullness of life and spiritual flourishing is little more than the careful shepherding of individuals through an historic set of well-worn and formulaic activities and requirements that seem almost predetermined to discourage and limit exploration beyond a safe and rather dull and featureless spiritual terrain. All too frequently Christian teaching focuses entirely upon individual salvation, making few if any connections with global justice issues or with ethical action in the real world. Moreover, the arcane language and clichéd terminology of its expression means that Christian teaching holds little if any attraction for outsiders and fails to articulate and stretch the experience, or release the full spiritual potential, of even committed Christian disciples.

This tendency to diffuse spiritual aspiration and prevent it from nurturing mature self-reflective individuals, or from engaging with the urgent needs of the world, has been characterized by psychiatrists and mental health professionals as creating "a false spirituality which traps people in narcissistic self-development" (Wilson, "Personal Care and Political Action," 1985, 173). Moreover, the churches themselves have given scant attention to the ways in which prayer can feed pathological tendencies and so be "psychologically … unhealthy" (Peter M. Gubi, *Prayer*, 2008, 37): creating unrealistic expectations and warped perceptions of reality. These are hard truths for church leaders to hear!

So it comes as no surprise that people outside the church are reluctant to consider, or use, the church as a resource for their spiritual development, or to give it responsibility for their spiritual flourishing, as they once did. And it is desperately sad, given all the resources and experience of prayer and spirituality that Christianity possesses, that the church does not show greater interest in listening to and supporting the spiritual aspirations of those—also called by God—who yet have no formal religious affiliation.

There has always been a much larger and more exciting range of expressions of spirituality and prayer within the world's religions than most of their adherents are ever aware of. A commitment to affirming the calling of all people into a relationship with the mystery of (what religious folk call) God will necessitate a still broader conception and tolerance of the immense diversity of forms that spiritual experience takes. If the church is to rise to the challenge of understanding and communicating meaningfully with the experiences of those who are in very different places on their spiritual journey, then it must be prepared to stand with one foot *outside* its rigid preconceptions of what is "orthodox" and "acceptable," and to listen attentively and respectfully to others if it ever wishes to be asked to share its own treasures and experience with them.

A New Sort of Church

It must be clear that this new understanding of vocation will necessitate a new sort of church. Jesus spoke of this himself, when he anticipates that the coming of the Spirit would rupture the established religious routines of his day:

> "No one puts new wine into old wineskins; otherwise, the wine will burst the skins, and the wine is lost, and so are the skins; but one puts new wine into fresh wineskins" (Mk 2:22; see also Mt 9:17 and Lk 5:37-38).

The safe "second nature" routines of church have smoothed the jagged edges of the gospel with a time-polished patina that reflects, not the radical image of Jesus, but the satisfying familiarity of our own faces. It is for this reason that Walter Brueggemann talks of Christians today as "living against the grain of our true vocation" (*Mandate to Difference*, 2007, 42) and hopes that the church will be able to accept the Spirit's invitation to move "beyond ourselves [and] the dominant script" (203), a script that James Alison characterizes as "the paralysed world of ecclesiastical half-truth" (*Faith beyond Resentment*, 2001 [2006], 210).

To move beyond this paralysis will be a risky undertaking; but then, this is generally the case with things of the Spirit. It will take a good deal of imagination too. So there will need to be a central place for daring and imaginative interpretations of Scripture, liturgy, and social action as the Spirit urges us on into that stage of liminality—that in-between space of dark unlearning before the twilight of possibility—that most of us need to inhabit before we can take the further leap out into what lies beyond.

It is here, in the semi-darkness before a new dawn, that we might at last hope to become receptive to hearing afresh the subversive gospel memories calling the church "out of its apathy, naïveté, and amnesia, and [drawing it] into dangerous new ground" (John Swinton, *Resurrecting the Person*, 2000, 127). But it will be far from easy for us.

An Impossible Future?

This morning I passed a church notice board showing a picture of an alarm clock and a caption asking whether "you'd like to wake up with Jesus in the morning?" I find it difficult to imagine that this sort of publicity is really going to connect with very many people. I fail to see how such language communicates very much that's positive or alluring: and certainly not the joy and urgency of the gospels to create a world of justice and full humanity for all people. I fail too to see how the idea of "waking up with Jesus" really serves to capture the imagination of anyone who is seeking spiritual meaning and enlightenment. It is sterile communication which trivializes the gospel and infantilizes people. Having said that, we shouldn't make too much of one random notice board!

But if the church is to have a creative role to play in the future, it needs to finally step away from all that is familiar, hackneyed, and trivial. It needs to start taking some risks and learn to live "beyond its borders" (Alistair McFadyen, *The Call to Personhood*, 1990, 29). We cannot escape the fact that Christian discipleship and ministry is an *ad-venture*: ever oriented to living the present well, and in generous openness to the future and to all that lies ahead. For the God revealed to us in Jesus is the one who makes possible what the world considers impossible. That God is calling each of us to action.

Time to explore!

Here are some ideas for you to discuss with friends in your local church or community:

- Beginning with the day of your birth, make a time chart or map of your own life. Extend the line back to the start of creation, for the atoms that make up your body were created then. Imagine God calling you into existence and giving you the unique vocation that is yours. What is this vocation? Share what you can with others in your church or network.

- List the various characteristics that make you a person. Include anything you like: your place of origin and family history; your hobbies, innate skills, and abilities. List whether you're left-handed, Spanish-speaking, able-bodied, gay, unemployed, bearded, widowed; or a vegetarian, sports fan, music lover, militant ecologist, civil rights campaigner, prone to ill heath, or a recent arrival in your town. Which of these characteristics are more valued by people? And which are more important to God?

■ Spend some time considering the truth that everyone is the same, precisely because everyone is different. How is this truth lived out in your church or local community?

Time for some action!

Here are some suggestions for you to try out:

■ Spend some time among the homeless, unemployed, street workers, and marginalized in your local community. Get to know them as individuals. What are they like? What do you learn from those that work among them about the nature of vocation and ministry?

■ Ask a group of church-goers or spiritual friends what they think their calling and life's purpose is. What can you discern about contemporary understandings of vocation?

■ Speak with folks in your congregation. What is the scariest thing they could imagine being asked to do for the gospel? List the commonalities and differences in what they say. Make sure to include your clergy and lay leaders.

■ What, or where, is the staleness in your church? What would your church have to do—how might it need to change—if it is to better connect with and serve your local community?

For church leaders:

- How would you describe your particular calling as a church leader? Do you have a particular expertise or gift? Do you use this, or does it lie forgotten and unused amid all the busy-ness of your work and the expectations of others?

- What makes you glad and excited about being a church leader? What aspects of the role do you find uncomfortable? How do you experience the expectations of those who would put you on a pedestal of moral perfection?

- What could your church learn from its community? What future you do foresee for your church, locally and nationally?

CHAPTER 2

Taking Time Out

Part 1: Stepping over the Threshold

Crossing the Threshold

The exact purpose of the raised step, door sill, or threshold in old houses and buildings is disputed. It may have served to keep the warm reed or chaff flooring inside; but it could equally function to keep out draughts and floodwater. Either way, the threshold marks the crossing point between the familiar safety of the indoors and the unknown danger of what lies outside. The "threshold" is the border between these two worlds, and its Latin equivalent gives us the term "liminal" (Latin "*limen*" and "*limitis*" meaning "border, boundary, or limits.")

The word liminal also signifies an in-between state or stage. In a performance, concert, or storytelling, during therapy, or even during a good sermon, the liminal describes that state of being or of attentive listening that the audience or congregation adopts when it relaxes, for a while, its focus on the concerns of daily life and "enters inside" the event.

From the point of view of the performer or preacher, this state is almost tangible. One can sense when those listening are occupying the liminal space between preacher and congregation. There they are, in the palm of your hand! From the point of view of the audience, people are "caught up" in what the performers are presenting. Consequently, there is a creative "coming together" or synergy in the liminal space, that has the capacity to affect people intellectually, spiritually, and emotionally: to change their perspective on things and move them into a new place.

At such times people often talk of "suspending their imagination," while others would say that it is *precisely through the use of their imagination* that they can enter this state or place at all; so perhaps it is better to talk of "suspending disbelief" or, more accurately, the ever-present critical faculty of our logical "left brain" thinking that insists on analyzing everything. This suspension permits things to move freely, "*sub*liminally," under the threshold of our critical faculties; for, despite the unquestioned value of human rational thinking, it is not the whole story of what makes us tick. Story, narrative, art, music, and poetry all speak their own visceral, emotional, and *subjective* truth that cannot be ignored or discounted.

There is also a clear argument to be made that liminal space can also be accessed by attentive reading or listening to the gospels themselves. A liminal space exists between the "back then" and the "here and now"; between the world of Jesus and his disciples and our own discipleship days. This is indeed the explicit intention behind the use of the "Ignatian" and "lectio divina" styles of Bible-based prayer that are popular today. The liminal space is where we might encounter fresh insights, discover the shortcomings of our previous thinking, and let go of our misconceptions so as to experience the healing affirmation and transforming guidance of the Spirit.

The Possibility of Change

It is well known that the majority of people in most congregations value the routine stability of their religious practices, asking few questions, and with little expectation other than that there will be worship at church the following Sunday. Change is not on their horizon. By contrast, there is both a small percentage of people in every congregation who are vehemently opposed to the possibility of change, and about an equal number who are always looking to identify and anticipate fresh thinking and innovation. Although all these people are called to discipleship, not all feel themselves called to change. They do not all associate their discipleship with the business of change.

Unfortunately, however, we no longer have the luxury of ignoring the need to change. We have to face up to it and embrace it; not only because change is inevitable and unavoidable, and not only because change is the place where we meet the living God; *but precisely because* it is the Spirit of God who is calling us to change!

Having the ability to discern and *work with* the transforming Spirit of God to purposefully create occasions for liminality is essential. Most people need to imagine, experience, or inhabit the "in-between" of the liminal before they can risk, or assent to, moving into what lies beyond the liminal space, and so change. It is in this sense that Walter Brueggemann talks of "liminality as a prerequisite for reappropriating life afresh" (Brueggemann, *The Word Militant*, 2007, 44). Good preaching, authentic liturgy, inclusive community, genuine pastoral care, attentive Bible reading, and a latent and keen sense of the aliveness and "presentness" of the living God all serve to create a Christian culture redolent with possibilities, potentiality, and promise. Such a liminal community is fresh thinking, outward looking, and future facing. Such a community takes creative risks for the gospel. Such a community steps outside together to explore the darkness of what is still—and perhaps forever— unknown, but which beckons us with its dazzling possibilities.

Here Be Dragons!

In truth, the Christian faith has never been fully comfortable with the idea of darkness. Those contemplatives and mystics who have explored it, and been transformed by it—Johannes Tauler, Marguerite Porete, Eckhart of Mainz, Mechthild of Magdeburg, John of the Cross, Edith Stein, to name but a few—have generally been marginalized, if not actively persecuted, by the church.

For most of us darkness is just that: dark, impenetrable, and scary. Because the idea of "dark" has come to embody the very opposite of the "light"—which, over centuries, we have imbued with rich connotations of safety, goodness, and salvation—we have almost entirely failed to properly and effectively investigate the nature of darkness. Darkness remains very largely a negative concept—a "black hole" in our belief—that we have filled with a nightmare scenario of evil, temptation, despair, suffering, doubt, and fear. We prefer to flee the darkness. We conceptualize darkness as threatening in its apparent emptiness; or else full of people, ideas, and experiences that we consider to be somehow dangerously "out of bounds" and implicitly detrimental to our spiritual well being. We correlate darkness with a dimension of our lives that we would rather ignore or forget. We associate darkness with the "abandonment by God" of Jesus on the cross and with a total absence of hope. We understand darkness to be the very antipathy of belief. And yet at the same time, we do something extremely odd, for we routinely consign people to this outer darkness! We banish into the darkness beyond the threshold all those whom we consider "unacceptable": all those whom we judge to be beyond or outside the parameters of *our* moral, religious, or cultural zone of familiarity and comfort. Whether it is those who offend us by their lifestyle, who threaten our sense of secure religious identity by their alternative religious outlook, or whose need makes too many demands upon our purse- and heart-strings. And this reaction, in turn, constantly reinforces the perceived negativity of the darkness to the point where, if we have to go "out there" at all, then we need to "take the light" with us!

Discovering the "Treasures of Darkness"

That is not to say that some light won't be readily welcomed by some of those "living in the darkness." It may just be that, in rushing in too eagerly with our light, we miss out on the opportunity to discover what Isaiah calls "the treasures of darkness" (Is 45:3). So what might this treasure be?

In answering this question we need perhaps to begin by remembering not only that the dark has been with us since before "The Beginning," but also that God is God of the darkness as well as of the light. God is equally at home in both the light and the dark, for:

> even the darkness is not dark to you;
> the night is as bright as the day,
> for darkness is as light to you (Ps 139:12).

Neil Douglas-Klotz (*The Hidden Gospel*, 1999, *passim*) points out that the "darkness"—Hebrew: "*hoshech*"—of Genesis 1:2 powerfully suggests the primordial, unstable, swirling chaos and churning potential within the *archetypal* (or pre-"Big Bang") time: a state rather like the "dream time" of the Australian aboriginal people. This state predates the linear space-time in which we live, and by which we make sense of our world. It is as utterly dark and unknowable as is our scientific knowledge of the what-if-anything was before the "Big Bang" or of the what-will-happen once our own sun dies.

According to Douglas-Klotz, light came into existence later in the biblical narrative when "God said, 'Let there be light' ("*aor*"); and there was light" (Gen 1:3). But the Hebrew word "*aor*" suggests a particular form or mode of enlightenment, thinking, or rationality. Not only that it was "light" and "light rays" which came into existence, but "all varieties of illuminating intelligence" (Douglas-Klotz, 75). This linear light, or "light ray" thinking of Genesis 1:3 can be characterized as straight-lined, logical, propositional: literally "prosaic." On the other hand, the primordial darkness ("*hoshech*") of Genesis 1:2 suggests latent potential; swirling, non-literal and imaginative forms of thinking. "Hoshech" is heuristic, open to multifarious random development and self-transcendence; literally "poetic" (from the Greek "*poietes*"), because it is ever suggestive of what is innately "pregnant with possibility."

Hence the "darkness" and "light" of Genesis become richly suggestive of alternative, if complementary, ways for us to inhabit and perceive the world. In having come to desire or prefer the linear, logical, and dualistic mode, we perhaps need to rediscover and value the older *wisdom of the darkness*: the mystical, metaphorical, poetic, non-linear ways of thinking, and of seeing the world, including our understanding of the church and its spiritual vision and ministry.

Letting the Darkness Illuminate Us

For just as, optically speaking, our human vision is confined to that rather small segment of the electromagnetic spectrum called visible light, so our spiritual vision needs to be extended to allow us to discern in the potent darkness both the "the promise within emptiness" (O'Leary, *Passion for the Possible*, 1998, 91) and the "wisdom of insecurity" (Watts, *The Wisdom of Insecurity*, 1976, cited in Willows and Swinton, 2000, 167).

We need to enter the darkness, not to banish it—or to "enlighten" whom or what we find there—but to learn to discern the diverse modes, colors, shades, and hues of which darkness really consists. We need to discover how to see in the dark by "enhancing our spectral range," how to think and learn about darkness from those whom we consider to be "living in darkness," and in so doing, how to better see as God sees. For it may well be that darkness is nothing like we conceive it to be. It may be that whom and what we find there have much to offer us and share with us. It may be that the darkness *is able to transform* our lives and our thinking in ways we had never conceived, or which our preference for the light has never permitted us to imagine.

Generally speaking we religious folk live our lives within the secure illumination of a fairly set world view. We have particular beliefs and values and use a mutually understandable Christian language. We create communities in our churches that operate according to a familiar logic or "hermeneutic": reassuring habits and disciplines that generate well-established forms of belief and pastoral care. It is not surprising, therefore, that we readily take for granted that what is "normal" and "enlightening" for us must be normal and enlightening for everyone else.

This is surely why many Christians prefer to stay with what we know. So if we visit churches of traditions other than our own, we find ourselves looking automatically for recognizable patterns to relate to and relax into. If we go to places of worship of the other world faiths—where little may make sense to us—we may consequently feel distinctly uncomfortable, and even perhaps fearful. And we need to remember that this same fear is felt by those who are not church-goers when they step across the thresholds of our own cherished Christian communities!

Yet part of the urgent task for risk-shaped Christian ministry is to help people lay aside a timid preference for the glow of the familiar and to engage with what is deeply and darkly *untried* and, consequently, with what is potentially disturbing and dislocating. This may be the "strange" beliefs and world views of our neighbors in the wider community, the practices of those people whose roots are from elsewhere in the world, or else the diverse life-styles of different generations.

Risk-shaped ministry is first and foremost about stepping outside our "timidity and traditionalism" (Willows and Swinton, 167), so as to *listen attentively and unconditionally* to our brothers and sisters, in the places where they are; *without* asking them to fulfill or conform to our own expectations and needs. We must learn to recognize that there are valid ways of understanding the world other than our own. And while we may rightly feel we have a great deal to say about things, our primary ministerial concern is to listen and learn to see reality through the eyes of our contemporaries.

This is a very Jesus-like calling; so it is also a deeply disturbing task. It requires us to confront what may be profoundly alien to us, or indeed to face up to what we'd prefer to ignore. Yet it is also the case that engaging with the darkness of our own ignorance and limitations will likely produce a rich alternative understanding of who, where, and how God is at work in the world.

Unlearning the Things We Take for Granted

There's a small but highly significant episode in the Gospels of Mark and Matthew where Peter attempts to offer Jesus what we might term "pastoral care." Jesus is telling his disciples that rejection, suffering, and death await him:

> Then he began to teach them that the Son of Man must undergo great suffering, and be rejected by the elders, the chief priests, and the scribes, and be killed, and after three days rise again (Mk 8:31; see also Mt 16:21).

Peter's response—not unlike our own, perhaps, when encountering someone talking about their own death—is to attempt to divert the thought, change the subject, or even silence Jesus. Peter "rebukes" Jesus: "Peter took him aside and began to rebuke him, saying, 'God forbid it, Lord! This must never happen to you'" (Mt 16:22; see also Mk 8:32). Jesus' reply is harsh: "'Get behind me, Satan!'" (Mk 8:33; see also Mt 16:23).

Why does Jesus call Peter "Satan?" Such a strong term, rarely used in the Hebrew Scriptures, (meaning "accuser" or "adversary," from a verb meaning to "oppose"), hints that Peter's well-intentioned words and reassuringly soothing pastoral approach stand in fundamental opposition to a new and as yet hidden reality.

This reality is revealed in Jesus' next words: "'For you are setting your mind not on divine things but on human things'" (Mk 8:33). To which Matthew adds: "'You are a stumbling-block to me'" (16:23).

This contraposition of "divine things" and "human things" suggests that a radically altered perception is demanded of those who would be disciples; a completely different way of looking at things: a new "gestalt," a radical transformation of intellectual, spiritual, and moral vision that is akin to, and as fundamental as, learning to see as well in the dark as we do in the light. For only this transformation will enable Jesus' disciples—then and now—to perceive and engage with the dynamic new approach to life required by the radically different values of the kingdom-kindom of God.

The New Testament is full of such "gestalts," stories of radical changes in perception. The encounter with the "Syrophoenician woman" (Mk 7:24-30), or "Canaanite woman" in Matthew's version (15:21-28), for instance, depicts Jesus as being brought up sharp by the disturbing realization that the old established boundaries and divisions between Jews and Gentiles, men and women, "us" and "them," were being breached. Consequently, he has to set about *unlearning* what are, for him, deeply familiar ways of knowing and being in the world.

Likewise, during his dark psychological dislocation—his "temptation"—in the wilderness (Mt 4:1-11; see also Lk 4:1-13), Jesus' solitary reflection on his baptism experience and its implications for his future require him to reconsider the normative and time-honored disciplines of power, and the extent to which he will have to negotiate them for himself. And as the devil seeks to lure Jesus into an easy acceptance of the received ways in which power operates—by its subtle assumption of the guise of relevance, effectiveness, and popular appeal illustrated in the three temptations—so Jesus has to make a supernatural struggle to escape the persuasive tug of the unquestioning logic of these conventional worldly mechanisms and behaviors. He has to do this in order to uncover the new "divine" rationale and his true destiny.

This same need to unlearn past experience and its "unquestioned common sense" is also at play during his dark anguish in the garden of Gethsemane. Here, even with his deep and constant intimacy with the ways of God, Jesus still has to realize that God might yet want a different and unknown outcome: "'My Father, if it is possible, let this cup pass from me; yet not what I want but what you want.'" (Mt 26:39; see also Mk 14:36). At the very moment of the imminent collapse of his world, Jesus has to find it within himself to lay aside all he has thus far learned about God's trustworthiness and risk relying unconditionally on the still-unexplored potency of the relationship itself, in order to help him cross over the threshold of human knowing into—and then through—the unknowable, unfathomable, realm of darkness.

Paul, too, along with all those who became disciples of Jesus, experiences the same unlearning of his inherited worldview. His encounter on the road to Damascus (Acts

9:1-9) results in three days of darkness: a liminal experience of physical and metaphorical blindness, in which both his identity is radically recast—as Saul becomes Paul—and a hitherto unthinkable new matrix is unveiled when the "scales fell from his eyes" (Acts 9:18). Once he emerges on the "other side" of the darkness, he encounters a vitally changed perception of reality that fundamentally reshapes his own life. And while, initially at least, it is far from easy for him, new energy, vision, wisdom, and courage are released that empower him to play the leading part in the exponential growth of the early Christian community.

Making Space for Creative Doubt

This liminal space between two realities—as we try to hold on to what has been and yet are drawn to reach out to what lies beyond us—is inevitably a time of uncertainty as the creative potency of newness agitates and chaffs against the familiar certainties that have given us strength and comfort in the past. This vacillation between two or more alternative possibilities is accurately captured in the word "doubt."

At such liminal moments as these, doubt enters the arena. And while many of us accept doubt—not quite knowing for sure—to be part and parcel of the whole framework of belief, for others it is the mortal enemy of faith, the worm that burrows away at the fabric of our souls and at those cherished certainties that give our lives meaning.

Whether we regard it as a welcome essential or an external interloper, doubt is an inherently and normatively destabilizing factor. It demands that we reconsider our assumptions. It requires us to take nothing for granted. Yet it also opens the door of our imagination to whatever may lie "beyond the darkness." And it urges us to step outside the "sure and certain hope" that may have accompanied our lives hitherto and to face the unknown.

This is an inherently risky, unstable, and insecure process in that, to some degree, it always contains the possibility of failure. We may fail to experience, feel, or hear anything at all. We may fail to discern any way forward. We may find ourselves simply at the beginning of a time of radical but necessary unlearning and "remaking"; a dark period of pregnant promise that is filled with the unavoidable pains of travail as something new is being created and brought slowly to birth.

Exploring the Wisdom of Insecurity

We may find ourselves being reduced to a fragile, helpless, and frustrating immobility while we await the revelation of what comes next, of the "yet-more" of God. But there is wisdom to be found in this insecurity; for doubt, unknowing, and unlearning are frequently the touchstones of startling novelty and creativity. This was true for Jesus in the wilderness as much as for Paul in Ananias' house. It is also true for today's disciples and for the institution of the church itself.

Engaging attentively and diligently with the pain of self-doubt, the disorientation of not-knowing, and with the need for authentic soul-searching offers real possibilities for the disclosure of newness. And at the end of the day it may well be, in Hauerwas' words, the only outcome "that Christians can rightly expect if their lives are truly lived in hope" (Hauerwas, *Performing the Faith*, 2004, 89).

Such a necessary process of introspective liminality, for today's disciples and church alike, leads inevitably to stillness and to silence in the darkness beyond the threshold. Being in such a location is hard to bear. It demands a peeling away of the layers of certainty and self-assuredness that have accrued over time; a willingness to be stripped of all that is comfortable and convenient; a letting go of the familiar habits of power and status; and a flexing of the inner resources of strength, trust, and grace so as to question and unlearn what we have assumed to be the ways and marks of God and, re-directed solely by the Spirit, come to encounter God afresh.

It is also entirely possible that, in taking this risk, we may find ourselves caught up in radical and astounding new beginnings.

Time to explore!

Here are some ideas for you to discuss with friends in your local church or community:

- If we are to be a new sort of church with a new sense of vocation, then what thoughts and habits might we have to "unlearn?"

- Which people does your church consign to the metaphorical darkness by its attitudes and practices? How might you begin to have a conversation about this?

- What are the things about yourself you feel God may be calling you to change? Share these thoughts with someone you trust.

Time for some action!

Here are some suggestions for you to try out:

- Persuade people from your church to spend time, alone or in pairs, in your local community. Go in the quiet morning, busy lunch time, or noisy evening. Sit still or walk quietly around and try to look beyond your Christian preconceptions to see through God's eyes. Where is there pain, suffering, and love? What creative things are happening? What might your church have to learn?

- Ask some local people who never or rarely attend church for their opinion of how and why the church might need to change. Just listen to what is said and don't try to defend the church. Take what you hear back for discussion.

- By yourself or with a friend, spend time sitting quietly outside in the darkness of a moonless night. What do you feel about the dark? What can you see in the dark that you've not seen before? What might it reveal to you about God?

For church leaders:

- In what ways have you changed during the time you have exercised a church leadership role? How have you experienced this change?

- What have been the times of darkness and unlearning for you as a church leader?

- What things have you discovered about God's call to take risks for the gospel?

Part 2: Breaking out into God's Newness

Confronting Our Fears

Elijah was afraid for his life as he fled from Jezebel after killing all the prophets loyal to the religious order she had established (1 Kings 19:1-3). Leaving even his servant behind, he hid in the wilderness and sat under a tree to await death. But God had other plans and, revived and restored by the ministrations of an angel, Elijah traveled a further forty days until he arrived at Mount Horeb (the sacred mountain of God, also called Sinai). From the cave in which he hides he is called forth to go and meet the living God. What happens next is familiar to us all:

> Now there was a great wind, so strong that it was splitting mountains and breaking rocks in pieces before the Lord, but the Lord was not in the wind; and after the wind an earthquake, but the Lord was not in the earthquake; and after the earthquake a fire, but the Lord was not in the fire; and after the fire a sound of sheer silence (11-12).

Elijah fails to detect God's presence in the ways that might be routinely expected of the Almighty: in the elemental wind, earthquake, and fire. But he does become unexpectedly aware of God in the "sheer silence" that follows. It is here, in this unearthly stillness, that Elijah finds himself overcome with awe and manages at last to hear God's voice. It is in the darkness and silence that Elijah is finally able to confront his fears about his life and ministry, and discern the shape of what he must do next in these perilous circumstances. It is in the silent darkness that Elijah encounters "[t]he promise within emptiness" (O'Leary, *Passion for the Possible*, 1998, 91).

A Promise Taking Shape

If silence and emptiness have a shape, then, according to O'Leary, it is inevitably cruciform (91). It takes this form because of the self-confrontation that lies at the heart of emptiness, darkness, and unknowing. Most of us—like Elijah—are usually unwilling to confront those areas of our being that are holding us back and preventing us from moving on. This is despite the fact that we are usually dimly aware, in the back of our minds, that God may well be found in the processes of interrogating our ego, its motivation, and its neediness. Confronting pain, ignorance, short-comings, and deliberate wrong choices and failures can be literally *excruciating.* (Indeed O'Leary talks of "[t]he Calvary of unmasking" [86].) So, if possible, we prefer to avoid both the pain and the simple inconvenience of having to examine ourselves, mend our ways, and begin afresh.

This is true for those involved in secular therapies and for each individual Christian in his or her discipleship. It is also manifestly true of the church as an institution. For in its contemporary sojourn in the wilderness of an ever-changing society and a world that no longer welcomes it entirely whole-heartedly, recognizes its authority, chooses to belong, or unquestioningly believe its doctrines, the church is experiencing an agonizing sense of failure, irrelevance, "out-of-touchness," and abandonment.

The church needs to recognize, accept, and integrate its own darkness within its self-understanding: both the dreadful errors of judgment it has made and the pain it has caused by its negative thinking and narrow pastoral practice. It needs to learn to accept that it has no monopoly on wisdom or holiness, and that it has much to learn from the wisdom and experience of others, whether or not these others "believe" or "belong" to a faith group or religious institution. In particular it needs to refocus its life and proclamation on the manner of Jesus' own journey of prophetic ministry; one that embodies and acknowledges, time and again, that God really is immensely more rich and complex than religious establishments ever imagine and teach. The church also needs to recognize that it cannot control the ways of God; that God has always been actively creative in the world outside its walls, and that God is calling us again to step outside and experience the new life that is being birthed.

If the church in the West is to experience the resurrection beyond its current crucifixion, then it must step courageously and creatively outside its confines and—without any ulterior motive or desire to "enlighten" others—learn to listen again to those people and things that it has forgotten, ignored, feared, or simply been unwilling to accommodate within its narrow field of vision and practice.

Rediscovering the Art of Listening

In his remarkable book, *The Art of Listening*, sociologist Les Back describes the need that sociology has, as a discipline, to embrace "the commitment to interpretation without legislation" (Back, 2007, 1). He suggests, in other words, that sociology must learn to offer interpretation without wishing either to prescribe the forms of interpretation, or to over-define the shape and content of human self-understanding and action. This idea has much to commend itself to the church. He continues:

> While the scale and complexity of global society may escape our total understanding, the sociologists can still pay attention to the fragments, the voices and stories that are otherwise passed over or ignored (1).

In particular he draws our attention to the fact that "the capacity to hear has been damaged and is in need of repair. This is what sociology is needed for, and, as a consequence, why it is a listener's art" (5).

If this is true of sociology, then how much more critically must it be true of the church's pastoral and prophetic ministry? For the church needs not only to reconnect with those who no longer attend, but to learn to listen hard—as did Elijah—for the voice of God in the experience of those who are silenced, in the dark, or ignored and who would never self-identify as Christians or, indeed, as believers of any sort. This task is as central to the future of the church as Back argues it is to that of theory and practice of sociology.

Note again the parallels in what Back writes here between the task of sociology and the church's ministry:

> [Sociological listening is] a form of openness to
> others that needs to be crafted, a listening for
> the background and the half-muted (8) … [an]
> attention to the hidden life of objects and places,
> the life that is either concealed within those objects
> or bleached from them by the formalities of power
> or the forgetfulness of conventional wisdom …
> a commitment to engagement, of opening up
> a sometimes very uncertain space of dialogue
> and encounter with people and their ordinary
> circumstances of life (9).

He continues: "our practices of listening … are implicated in grids of power and knowledge and as a result are deeply historical in character" (24), and "the challenge for sociology … is to develop a critique that captures life's light and heat (20) … in order to admit the excluded, the looked past, [and] to allow the 'out of place' a sense of belonging" (22).

In a similar vein, if the church is to stand a chance of being once again a vital community of meaning for those living in the West, then it needs to acknowledge the damage wrought by its overwhelmingly historical norms of interpretation and its lack of openness to the contemporary lived experience and existential joys and dilemmas of ordinary people. The church needs to look beyond its own "formalities of power and conventional wisdom" in order to open up that creative if "uncertain space for dialogue" of which Back speaks, if it is ever to be able, in a paraphrase of his words, to be touched by "the light and heat of life" which Christians call the Spirit of God.

The time is ripe for the church to step outside its comfort zone—its easy habits of historical acquired power—and shape new forms of pastoral and prophetic ministry that seek to *listen to and affirm* the spiritual quests, drives, and longings of *all* people, and so create the rich sense of belonging in the world that is so desperately needed in the West.

Spirituality in the Marketplace

Something of what this might mean can be glimpsed in the account of Paul's visit to Athens (Acts 17:16-34). According to Luke's account, the Athenians appear to be a cosmopolitan people familiar with the presence of "foreign divinities" (17:18). Indeed their "city was full of idols" (16), and competing Jewish, Epicurean, and Stoic theologies and philosophies (17). When Paul begins to preach the resurrection of Jesus, he is taken before the city elders on the Areopagus both to give an account of himself, and also, it seems, to indulge the contemporary passion for "telling or hearing something new" (21).

It doesn't take much reading between the lines to paint a remarkably modern picture of a people deeply intrigued by an eclectic mix of "idols" (16), religious "objects of worship" (23) made "of gold, or silver, or stone … [or] image[s] formed by the art and imagination of mortals" (29). There is even "an altar with the inscription, 'To an unknown god'" (23). It is this altar that opens up a space for Paul to talk about Jesus: "'What therefore you worship as unknown, this I proclaim to you'" (23).

It is, of course, impossible to know from the biblical text the real extent of Paul's engagement with what he finds. He does tell the Athenians, "I see how extremely religious you are in every way" (22). He "looks carefully at the objects of [their] worship" (23). He even quotes some snippets from the *Phaenomena* of the Greek philosopher Aratus (an astrological work about the stars and planets) and from writings in honor of Zeus by the famously tattooed philosopher-seer Epimenides: "For 'In him we live and move and have our being'; as even some of your own poets have said, 'For we too are his offspring'" (28). It is clear that Paul regards *with all seriousness* the religious strivings he finds among the citizens and visitors to the city.

It is not possible to know for sure the impact *on Paul* of what he sees: for his concern is only to faithfully preach the gospel of Jesus. But what is evident from the text is that the idea of the resurrection was the cause of considerable disbelief and scoffing (32). Even alongside all the gaudy glitter and razzmatazz of cosmopolitan Athenian worship, that particular idea was, for many, one step too far. Only a few people were converted and Paul left.

New Ways of Seeing

These are not new observations (see Biddington, "Spirituality in the Market-place" 2007), but they do emphasize the challenges of getting people to look afresh at how they see the world and to be open to imagine things differently. This is just as true for those in the church who would wish to identify and engage with new forms of belief and practice, of "being and doing." This is—remarkably— despite the fact that the church is meant to be a community where God's newness is *ever actively discerned.*

We seem too often to have forgotten that, because we believe that God is a constantly self-revealing God, the church is, therefore, *supposed to be* a community of people who are passionate about—and committed to—the task of seeing how and where God is at work. It may be in ways and terms we recognize by their reliable familiarity or, indeed, on those occasions when the shape and manner of the revelation may surprise, shock, or even scare us. While we are rather good at recognizing the former, we need urgently to risk acquiring the knack of learning the latter.

Learning to perceive and explore the startling novelty of God's self-revelation in the people and places outside our churches, and being alert to the myriad epiphanies that happen there with amazing regularity, is akin to the gestalt-oriented approach used by some counselors and psychotherapists.

A gestalt approach "[seeks] the unexpected and the new while using the supportive structures of the past" (Clarkson, *Gestalt Counselling in Action,* 1989, 25). It aims to empower the individual to live authentically and responsibly in the present while looking to the future and anticipating new insights and growth. It assumes her basic healthiness while encouraging her to be creative and take risks so as to better respond to her needs and the needs of those around her.

Central to a gestalt approach is the "figure/ground" paradigm, whereby the "ground" is the individual's background belief system, and the "figure" is her lived experience. The therapy operates by enabling her to move between the two—or to "foreground" the experience, issue, or idea—and so acquire some critical distance or inspired insight that enables her to move forward into a new state of being or believing. But—critically—in bringing what is new to the fore, she has to raise her eyes off the background *in order to see what is new:* and so come to appreciate (or relate to) the background differently. She has to cross a threshold, enter a liminal space and a time of darkness or doubt, before the new stage or insight becomes clear.

In this way gestalt therapy can be seen as a way of managing the loss of old, outgrown, or now unhelpful attitudes, and of inviting people to imagine, perceive, and explore new horizons and frontiers.

A New Impetus for the Church

It is then possible to see that the church itself is called to be a kind of "medium for gestalt." For if the "ground" is the historic tradition of interpretation and belief, then the "figure" is the experience—now—of God, the divine, and our response to the mystery of life. And so the task for, and vocation of, the church is to be a place where such liminal, learning and unlearning, experience is encouraged and valued, and where interpretation and empowerment are learned from, and offered and shared within, the wider community. This impetus then serves to further resource both the life and ministry of the church, and also the on-going enrichment of its collective wisdom, and the practical expression of this in the light of the unending self-revelation of God.

In this model there is a fluid interchange between those who follow the way of Christian discipleship and those fellow travelers and seekers who, from different perspectives "outside" the church, have—nonetheless—valuable lived experience to share.

The problem is that, notwithstanding its rhetoric, the church has mostly *not* lived out its commitment to being an inclusive and outward facing community. Even despite Paul's startlingly radical insight that "in Christ Jesus you are all children of God" (Gal 3:26) and "there is no longer Jew or Greek, there is no longer slave or free, there is no longer male and female; for all of you are one in Christ Jesus" (28). Indeed, the church appears to have given up on this vision fairly early in its history (and *permanently*, once it became the established imperial religion), and has remained ever since institutionally hierarchical and inherently gendered, inflexible, intolerant of difference, and very rigidly boundaried.

While the church has traditionally called itself the "Body of Christ," this body metaphor is an essentially static one. For notwithstanding that a body can indeed grow and change, the church's historic use of the metaphor has ultimately failed to facilitate the personal transformation-within-community that Jesus seems to have held as the basis of his own prophetic ministry (see Biddington, *Risk-Shaped Discipleship*, 2010, 141-144). While the idea of the church as body does imply community and relationality as an essential part of the process of finding "fullness of life" (Jn 10:10), it fails to really enable the practical application of Jesus' vision of radical equality to happen. It did not, for instance, in any way enable the early church to speak out against slavery or the discrimination against its more "inferior member(s)" (1 Cor 12: 24). Nor does it enable those in today's church who are still made to feel second class—Paul's "less respectable members" (1 Cor 12:23)—to feel fully acceptable to and representative of the church and its ministry.

While we should not unduly stretch this or any metaphor too far, it nevertheless follows that, if the church is to continue using it as part of its rhetoric, then it needs to think about how—by extension—the body's "skin" and "thresholds," its points of entry and exit, its structures, limits, and boundaries, can be made more porous and flexible, more genuinely welcoming, inclusive, empowering, healing, and transformative.

On Becoming a Vine

A better metaphor for the church is that of the vine with its implications of sameness and equality, mutuality, and common life. For ultimately we are all just fruit of the vine that is Jesus, nurtured equally by God the vine grower and by the ground in which God has planted us. Yes—critics may say—some of the vine's branches will be cut off and burned (Jn 15:6), but at least all have the same opportunity to flourish.

For the vine is a non-hierarchical organic entity. It models the integrated being of God, on which we are all equally dependent for our nourishment. In this model we find expressed our inter-dependence insofar as are we aware of the way we stand side by side in needful and creative solidarity with our neighbors, and give each other the space and encouragement we need to become fruitful individuals in the one community. As grapes together on the same vine, we share a closeness and awareness of each other's situations and, by touching each other, we begin to give expression to the idea of our being an integral whole. This whole is a porous, permeable, flexible, and mutual organism: where each fruit is in intimate living contact with the others and sustained equally by God.

The metaphor is also apposite in that the vine receives its nourishment from *outside* itself, from the ground, the context, in which it/we have been planted. It is nourished from the soil—"*ha adamah*" in Hebrew, symbolically "earth" and "man"—and from the human community, the dirt-filled potential of humanity—that surrounds and sustains the vine and in which it grows.

This idea is beautifully illustrated by U.A. Fanthorpe in her poem "Friends' Meeting House, Frenchay, Bristol" where she describes how the vine begins to grow only: "when the lovely holy distractions, / Safe scaffolding of much-loved formulae, / Have been rubbed away;" (*Neck Verse*, 1992, 47). It is when the familiar routines of church have been discarded to give the vine the ground in which to root and flourish. She continues:

> And the herb is the Vine, savage marauder,
> That spreads and climbs unstoppably,
> Filling the house, the people, with massing insistent shoots
> That leaf through windows and doors, that rocket through chimneys,
> Till flesh melts into walking forms of green,

Trained to the wildness of Vine, which exacts
Such difficult witness; whose work is done
In hopeless places, prisons, workhouses,
In countinghouses of respectable merchants,
In barracks, collieries, sweatshops, in hovels
Of driven and desperate men.
It begins here in the ground of silence.

What is needed then is a mechanism that allows the vine to take root, be nurtured, and flourish "insistently" so as to enable the church to be carried out beyond itself and engage effectively with the world outside its walls. What might this mechanism be?

The Church as Open Therapeutic Community

The church must become the kind of rooted, and hence "radical," dynamic egalitarian community that is able to see itself less as an inherently hierarchical "body," where the "lesser members" are benignly welcomed but ultimately not encouraged or enabled to find—or offer—transformation. Instead of a community where a "foot" will always be a "foot" and where most males always assume themselves to be the "head," it must become one that is genuinely empowering and transformative for *all its members.*

Here the church becomes an exciting, vibrant community where authentic spirituality and the things of God are encouraged and explored for the benefit of all. In this church, "authority" is expressed in a genuine and unconditional commitment to nurture the humanity of all people: regardless of their birth, upbringing, identity, or life history.

Here the church becomes a *therapeutic* community where people offer their experience, time, passion, wisdom, and energy for the healing and support of others: a "Christic" or Christ-like community able to "recover the joyous possibilities

of our interconnected selves" (Grey, *Sacred Longings*, 211).
Here the church becomes radically and insistently open to
all that is outside and beyond itself, so as to discover its own
path to self-transformation and to a fundamentally different
kind of ministry.

A New Sort of Ministry

The New Testament talks eloquently of the various kinds
of ministry that the early Christian community received,
created, and valued, in response to its desire to communicate
with the world in which it found itself. In Ephesians we read:

> The gifts he gave were that some would be apostles,
> some prophets, some evangelists, some pastors and
> teachers, to equip the saints for the work of ministry,
> for building up the body of Christ, until all of us come
> to the unity of the faith and of the knowledge of the
> Son of God, to maturity, to the measure of the full
> stature of Christ (4:11-13).

While writing to Christians in Corinth Paul identifies,
"first apostles, second prophets, third teachers; then deeds
of power, then gifts of healing, forms of assistance, forms of
leadership, various kinds of tongues" (1 Cor 12:27-29).

Famously, he then goes on to challenge these organized
categories of ministry with the hint of a yet "more excellent
way":

> Are all apostles? Are all prophets? Are all teachers?
> Do all work miracles? Do all possess gifts of healing?
> Do all speak in tongues? Do all interpret? But strive
> for the greater gifts. And I will show you a still more
> excellent way (12:29-31).

This *new* way is so wonderfully elucidated in his eulogy about love that it is popular at wedding ceremonies (1 Cor 13). But the primary importance of Paul's words for today's church is neither the relationship between two individuals on their wedding day, nor the relationships within the Christian community at large. For the idea of a "more excellent way" of Christian ministry stands as a challenge for us to create new and essentially daring forms of loving service and ministry through which we might respond to God's calling us to risk reconnecting with, and learning from, the world and the universe around us.

Time to explore!

Here are some ideas for you to discuss with friends in your local church or community:

- Do you think that the authority of the church manifests in past revelation, traditions, and models of leadership? Or by virtue of the belief, hope, and trust given to it by believers down the centuries?

- What is essential for the church? Does this change over time? What attitudes and behaviors might the church need to let go of in order to reconnect with people in today's world?

- The church has been likened to both a vine and the Body of Christ. Which metaphor do you think better fits the church today?

Time for some action!

Here are some suggestions for you to try out:

- What is your understanding of therapy and healing? Alone or with friends, walk around your neighborhood to see what healing activities you can find.

- What creative ideas, groups, and initiatives are emerging in your local community? How do you see God active in them?

- How might your church learn from what is happening in your local community?

For church leaders:

- How do you understand and use the authority that has been given you? How might you exercise or embody it differently?

- How might your church and congregation change in response to what God is doing in your local community? What co-operative strategies can you identify and put into place?

CHAPTER 3

Relearning the "Three R's": Re-Imagining, Reconnecting, Re-Enchanting

Part 1: The Church and Contemporary Religiosity

An Easy Fiction

There are many voices in the West saying that secularism has fully come of age and has successfully marginalized the church and all that it stands for: its stories, practices, and values, as well as its often historically privileged status in society. Many commentators point to the much-publicized views of "new atheists" like Richard Dawkins as providing the "only" intellectually, scientific, and incontrovertibly "truth-full" reading of reality. They claim that this has eliminated every vestige of credibility from the "superstitious fictions" pedaled by believers the world over. They also frequently cite how religious adherence and regular attendance in churches—and also in synagogues, temples, gurdwaras, and even mosques—has declined exponentially in the last half century, on either side of the Atlantic.

To imagine in this way that religion is all over and done with is an easy fiction. The more complex reading suggests that religion—the religious impulse—seems to respond in some fundamental way to the indefatigable urge within "Human Beings" to imagine the world differently and better than it is. Sure, "better" for ourselves: since we remain profoundly ego-centric. But "better" too—in our more inspired moments and dreams—for all people everywhere:

more inclusive, equitable, and just. This is a vision of a humanity we can all aspire to, and which right now the world urgently needs to witness in action.

Uncomfortable Change

It is also very clear both that the church has yet to respond effectively to this challenge, and that there are opportunities for it to play a remarkably potent and effective role in western society. If we are prepared to listen hard, then it is still possible to hear an irresistible call to prophetic action and ministry. But the church has to be willing to lay aside its pathological fear of change and risk, and work creatively with God to take advantage of these opportunities.

Unfortunately, many Christians fall into the trap of imagining that the church is something apart from us, distinct from us, and over which we have no influence or control. This is despite the fact that the gospels clearly suggest that it is we who are the Body of Christ, and we who are the vine. The gospels suggest that the church *is more us*—the baptized people of God—than it is those individuals who have traditionally seen themselves to be "in authority over us"; that the church *is more its living disciples* than it is those institutional structures, protocols, and hierarchies that appear never to change or develop over the course of long centuries, and whose voice has often been confused with divine revelation itself. It is imperative, at this point in our history, that we remember this if we want to fulfill our God-given vocation to serve the world.

Discerning the Spirit Stirring amid the Chaos

The second decade of this century were years that are destined to be remembered for their global demonstrations of social unrest, political revolution, religious discord, rapid change in the economic markets, and widespread personal disquiet and despair with the world order. There were protests in both the US and the UK against the mismanagement of the banks and currency markets, and against the popularly perceived profiteering by "fat cats" working in our financial centers. Temporary protest camps arose outside stock exchanges and around cathedrals. There were riots in major cities and, of those arrested for vandalism and looting, the majority were first-time offenders, and largely unemployed young men.

Further analysis seems to suggest that the profound hunger and *dis*-ease of many of these young people was driven by a desperate desire for success and fame. It was fuelled by the visible excesses of a celebrity "get rich quick" culture— witnessed nightly on our TV screens—that offers immense instant rewards to those who have the good fortune to go to particular schools, receive unearned and unmerited life-changing opportunities, or have the "luck" to be spotted or noticed by someone in the press or media.

On one reading, these young people claim naively that "life is unfair." They want to be rich and famous, to be instantaneously recognized in the streets, to be "cool." They want to feel they can "be somebody," and be admired or envied in their turn. And they seem to be prepared to do almost anything to get what they feel is their due. On another reading, however, they simply want security and to be able to have dreams and aspirations that might just have a chance of being fulfilled, despite life's unfairness. They want to be taken seriously as members of society and to witness and celebrate their own contribution. They want to belong. But they don't know how to belong or where to look for clues, role models, and "heroes." Some may, of course, have fewer life chances than others, but—more critically—most appear to have no meaningful and resilient philosophical or spiritual framework upon which to build or articulate their aspirations.

It is not just our young people. For decades, sociologists of religion have drawn our attention to the phenomenon of the "churched," the "un-churched," and the "de-churched." They point out a steady decline: from church attendance to non-attendance; from knowledge of the Christian faith to disinterest; and then to the perceived utter irrelevance of the church for so many people today. Consequently, they also speak of a steady increase in those who are looking elsewhere for meaning, some of whom will have turned to other faiths or forms of religiosity and some of whom are failing to find any meaning or spiritual fulfillment anywhere.

Yet, through the thwarted longings of all of these people, the Spirit of God is speaking: calling the followers of Jesus to step outside their structures and institutions and engage with the hopes and aspirations of those outside our churches. And while the church in so very many places has a remarkable track-record of social engagement, of transforming communities and the lives of many ordinary people, it has very often not succeeded in engaging effectively, creatively, or unconditionally with the unfulfilled spiritual needs and aspirations of those outside its doors.

Claiming a New Ministry for the Church

The relentless and world-changing progress of science over several centuries has resulted in two quite distinct, if complementary, scientific and religious methodologies and understandings of the universe. We are today at a place in our history where the church can, if it chooses, risk letting go any remaining and unnecessary preoccupation with the "objective truth" of scientists and religious fundamentalists alike, and opt instead to help people to discover and name the truth of our *spiritual* nature and needs, and so work to celebrate the astonishing longing and creativity of the human spirit.

For it is precisely this deep spiritual need and desire that is everywhere manifest in the hopes, fears, aspirations, and actions of so many people. It is precisely this potential for spiritual aliveness and creative action that lingers—so often untapped—in the lives of both Christian disciples and non-churchgoers alike. Finding a dynamic response to this spiritual need is the unquestionable and urgent vocation of the church and its ministry today.

It is important to emphasize, though, that it is essentially a *spiritual and ethical* vocation, and not a religious one, that the church needs to fulfill. The ministry of the church is not chiefly to preach belief, important though this is for many. The task facing the church is to help people to a robust exploration of their spiritual longings, desires, experiences, and identity, and to the creation of an authentic spirituality and ethical practice that enables people to discover and experience the wonder of being alive and the intimacy of our relationship with each other and with the universe that is our home.

It is crucial to undertake this ministry in the frank recognition that authentic religious and spiritual experience is not the sole privilege of church-goers or religious believers. For whether or not they attend a religious institution or have a formal religious affiliation or orthodox beliefs, people of all kinds do, in fact, have genuine experiences of the "sacred" or "spiritual" in a wide variety of forms. Often, though, they lack any framework for interpreting and integrating it into their daily living.

These experiences may overlap with "mainstream" religious ones. They may also—quite likely—be inspired by a combination of several different models or archetypes drawn from disparate sources; or they may be complete "one-offs," unique to an individual and to her interaction with contemporary culture. What is critically important is for the church to find ways of engaging with these myriad experiences in the knowledge that there will be *at least as much* to learn as there are things to share. For the nurture and interpretation of authentic spiritual experience and exploration is as central to the need for human, social, and global regeneration as it is fundamental to the church's contemporary vocation and ministry.

A God of One's Own

Ulrich Beck's remarkable book *A God of One's Own* (2010) takes as its thesis the idea that, after one of the bloodiest centuries of human history, the widespread loss of meaning and purpose, and the systemic failure of the institutional church in the West, there has been an increasing tendency for people to create "a God of one's own."

Contrary to what we might imagine, Beck is adamant there is no inevitability that, in doing this, people will simply resort to making a "god in their own image." We can all remember those times when we have allowed ourselves to imagine God as a "Father Christmas figure" rewarding us when we're good, or as a "stern judge" punishing evil doers, or as a "puppet master" pulling the strings of people's lives and destinies. And it is no doubt true that this will indeed be exactly the sort of god that some people will always tend to create, given half a chance. God will simply become a mechanism for wish-fulfillment, or for meting out punishment on those we might identify as meriting their "just rewards." And when this happens, God will indeed be tamed, domesticated, and trivialized, as has so often been the case.

Beck's argument is much more complex and persuasive. He begins by citing the story of Etty Hillesum. A non-practicing Jew caught up in the horrors of the Nazi invasion of Holland, she worked initially in a local transit camp to

alleviate the distress of those awaiting deportation, before
also being sent to her death. In her letters and journal, she
records her thoughts and feelings about her life experiences
and her conversations with God.

What emerges for Hillesum is that, in contemplating the
joys and sorrows of her life, her dire predicament, and likely
murder, she makes a profound personal discovery about the
nature of God. That God is very different from how religious
groups have generally taught. She learns that God requires
neither creeds nor dogmas, neither formal worship nor
endless praise. That God is not bound by human constraints
and is happy to be set free to be a very different God: even
if this means that God is consequently misunderstood and
rejected by established institutions and belief systems.

During her last months, Hillesum encounters—or rather
is encountered by—a God who enables her to find her true
self, and so achieve self-transcendence. In the course of
deeply meaningful conversations with God, she discovers that
God is woven into the fabric of life and inescapably bound
up with, and not external to, the particularities of human
existence. This enables her to discover the connections
between her own life and the nature of life itself. She locates
herself, and finds her meaning, in the events of each moment.
She comes to know a God who is not omnipotent and who
cannot be called upon to dramatically or magically rescue
her from her fate or fulfill her dreams and desires for an
alternative future, the kind of God that is often created
by people in their times of need. Rather she learns—very
uncomfortably—that God obliges her to take responsibility
for herself, her actions, and her situation, and to let go of fear.
Indeed, Hillesum discovers that, in this God, there is no fear.

In particular, she is nourished by the disclosure of the
fragility of God—because God is ever the "questioner who has

no answers" (Beck, 2010, 9). This enables her to see and love the beauty and fragility of existence, humanity, and the world for what it is. Critically, she discovers how much God needs people; that it is not God who—as we imagine—rescues us, but we ourselves who need to continually rescue God from the institutional and doctrinal imprisonment in which God has been bound.

Can the Church Affirm Such a God?

Beck argues that, if Hillesum's discovery of "a God of her own" is one that is made possible by—or is the product of—centuries of secularization in the West, then it may indeed prove to be of the greatest relevance for our time. For such an understanding of "God" helps heal the division, the popularly conceived "unbridgeable chasm," between the worlds of belief and non-belief which has been created by the gradual emergence of the ever narrower and more divisive notion that faith is simply a subjective fiction that can be outgrown and dismissed by the rigors of "objective scientific truth." Such an understanding of "a God of one's own" recreates and reaffirms the solidarity between *all* people who desire to see a better world: regardless of whether or not they happen to have a religious belief. It broadens out the idea of "God" to include wider perceptions and experiences of the nature of human life, values, and aspirations, and the possibility of spiritual meaning-making for all people.

What better ministry, then, for the church, than to work to affirm this quest for "a God of one's own" in all people and in all communities everywhere. For the idea of such a radical and prophetic task sketches out the very real possibility of a reinvigorated and transformed Christian ministry: one that is able to make deep, creative, and empowering connections with people everywhere.

What of Jesus?

The deeply transgressive nature of Jesus' teaching
and prophetic action is, these days, once again being
fully recognized. While he remained a faithful Jew and
fully committed to the revelation of God in the Torah, he
nonetheless gave evidence for a robustly individualistic
approach to his relationship with God. But is it too much to
then claim that he also created a "God of his own"?

It is only in Mark's Gospel that Jesus is recorded as using
the name "abba"—"daddy"—when speaking with God: "He
said, 'Abba, Father, for you all things are possible'" (14:36).
But the fact that this Aramaic term is actually retained in the
scriptural text alongside the Greek word for "Father" suggests
something of its importance for Mark and the early church in
characterizing Jesus' relationship with God.

While we must be mindful of claiming that Jesus was
necessarily unique in using the word "abba"—for there is
evidence that some of his contemporaries also used the
term—it does suggest a spiritual intimacy with God that was
unusual and uncommon within the Jewish tradition of Jesus'
day and earlier. (References to God as "father"—though not
"abba"—are found less than twenty times in the entire Jewish
Bible.) But it is very clear that Jesus habitually called God
"abba," and that this was remembered and imitated by the
early Christian community:

> For you did not receive a spirit of slavery to fall back
> into fear, but you have received a spirit of adoption.
> When we cry, "Abba! Father!" it is that very Spirit
> bearing witness with our spirit … (Rom 8:15, 16).

> And because you are children, God has sent the Spirit
> of his Son into our hearts, crying, "Abba! Father!"
> (Gal 4:6).

It is also clear that the gospel writers portray Jesus as understanding himself to be relationally bound to God as a son to his father:

> "My Father, if it is possible, let this cup pass from me; yet not what I want but what you want" (Mt 26:39).

> He said to them, "Why were you searching for me? Did you not know that I must be in my Father's house?" (Lk 2:49).

> "The Father and I are one" (Jn 10:30).

It is apparent, too, that this self-understanding was the source of much contention with his critics:

> For this reason the Jews were seeking all the more to kill him, because he was not only breaking the sabbath, but was also calling God his own Father, thereby making himself equal to God (Jn 5:18).

Time and again—in brief exchanges and in the extended discourses of John's Gospel—Jesus is remembered as exploring the idea of the father-son relationship, and using it to give a particular character to his understanding of himself and of his relationship with God. He eschews the formal hierarchical language of the established Jewish liturgical and scriptural traditions—Almighty, Lord, King—and opts instead for a frame of reference and a language that serve to make God and the divine more real to him.

All three accounts of his baptism suggest that, from the moment he rose out of the waters of the Jordan, he had discovered his connection with the divine creator:

> And just as he was coming up out of the water, he saw the heavens torn apart and the Spirit descending like a dove on him. And a voice came from heaven, "You

are my Son, the Beloved; with you I am well pleased."
(Mk 1:10-11; see also Mt 3:16-17 and Lk 3: 21-22).

Throughout his itinerant life, from the Jordan to
Golgotha, it is this one central point of connection, this one
intimate and abiding relationship with *"abba* God," that
sustains him on his journey. It is this atypical, and for some,
deeply offensive characterization of God's relationship with
humanity that seems to have been key to what we might
call Jesus' life-sustaining spirituality. Very few others had
conceived of their connection to God in this way; but, over
time, it became as significant a part of early Christian identity
as it had been for Jesus.

What of Us?

While the charge of Jesus "making himself equal to God"
(Jn 5:18) was, and remains, a blasphemy within Judaism, so,
in a similar way, the idea that Jesus might be said to have
created a "God of his own" will seem to some today to fulfill
the fears of "orthodox" Christians about people making God
in their own image. But if the individualistic language of
father-son relationality made God more real for Jesus, and if
we, too, are desirous of promoting the same authentic life-
affirmation in our world, then we must surely need to find
forms of ministry that encourage the contemporary quest
to discover and explore effective and meaningful forms of
spiritual language and practice.

Christianity has changed and developed. So has the
church. We need to do so again if we are to fulfill our primary
vocation. We must risk stepping outside all that has become
dull, stale, clichéd, energy-sapping, and unappealing to find
ways of recreating authentic language, metaphors, concepts,
rituals, practices, and forms of self-belief and understanding
that enable people to re-imagine their place in the world,

reconnect with their true selves and with their neighbors, and discover again the staggering awareness that God's universe is full of enchantment, mystery, radical amazement, and breathtaking possibility.

Time to explore!

Here are some ideas for you to discuss with friends in your local church or community:

- Who is the church for you and what is your role in it?

- What signs do you see of the spiritual hunger at the heart of so much contemporary social unrest?

- Who is God for you?

- What do you make of the idea that the church's ministry is to encourage authentic spiritual exploration?

Time for some action!

Here are some suggestions for you to try out:

- Organize a discussion with some Christian and non-Christian friends on the subject: If there were a God, who or what would God be?

- With the same group, compile an informal questionnaire about what people in your community feel gives their lives spiritual meaning, depth, beauty, hope, and fulfillment. Share the results with as many people as possible.

- Then find ways of exploring how people in your community are connected to each other and to the universe.

- Compile a list of things in your community that people feel need putting right or improving. Devise creative strategies for achieving some of these.

For church leaders:

- Organize an anonymous poll of your congregation's understandings of God: the language (titles, adjectives), feelings, and images they associate with God. Share the results together.

- Devise a workshop on "What makes us spiritual and ethical creatures?" to explore the idea of "a God of one's own." Be sure to involve non-church attendees from the local community.

- What questions do you have of your own understanding of God? What does the "yet-more" of God look or feel like for you?

Part 2: Re-Imagining, Reconnecting, Re-Enchanting

If you have worked through these last exercises, you will have been struck by the need to have imagination! Since God is, to paraphrase St Anselm, greater than anything we can conceive "logically," then the need to use our imaginative faculties is essential if we wish to help people to reconnect with "God"; however they might conceive "him" or "her."

Some of us, however, regard the imagination as deeply disturbing: especially when it is used in a theological or spiritual context. This is because of its popular, if superficial, confusion with fantasy. But there is a clear difference between the two. For fantasy takes us to where we want to go. It closes off and limits future options to merely fulfilling the outcomes and scenarios that we desire. We remain in control. Imagination opens up the present and the future to multiple outcomes and possibilities. It takes us to places we had not foreseen.

Consequently, while it is always a risky undertaking, it is also a deeply spiritual and "prayer-full" practice. For just as prayer is ultimately about trying to see the world through God's eyes, and responding, so our imagination is that bit of our psyche that is most readily able to connect with the proactive and ever-generative Spirit of God swirling or burrowing through the darkness, just beyond our current viewpoint and outside our immediate understanding.

Imagination offers fresh "possibilities of interpretation" and not just "new meanings" and is "central to the Christian life" (Hauerwas, *Performing the Faith*, 2004, 129 and 93). Imagination "*unveils* the hidden reality" (Henry Corbin quoted in Wink, *The Human Being*, 2002, 40), is "the sole organ capable of conveying" overwhelming truth, and "enable[s] us to experience God" (Wink, 160 and 259).

Imagine then, if you will, a Christian ministry whose key focus is to nurture the imagination of those church attendees and non-attendees living together in the local community. How is such a radical ministry to be imagined? What would a new sort of "religious imagination" look like, and achieve, in our churches and communities?

On Re-Imagining

Re-Imagining Things into Reality

Jesus himself was nothing if not imaginative. Time and again his use of parable serves not only to excavate fresh meanings from everyday objects, stories, and incidents but, in stretching, subverting, and transgressing traditional

and accepted norms of interpretation, it also empowers his
listeners to use their own imaginations as a tool to transform
their knowledge of the ways of the "kingdom-kindom" of
God.

I have explored elsewhere the subversive functioning of
Jesus' "parabolic imagination" to disrupt the *status quo*, prick
the bubble of "normal" thinking and behavior, and invite his
listeners to step into a new place (Biddington, *Risk-Shaped
Discipleship*, 2010, 152-169). Now I want to emphasize
the capacity of the imagination to create the liminal space
necessary for ushering in new understandings and possibilities
for Christian vocation, and for discerning tangible signs of
fresh options for the ministry of today's disciples.

Jesus and Imagination

There is a distinct possibility that the parables of Jesus
should best be read as simple storylines: as outlines or
short-hand notes that were—almost inevitably—varied
and modified by him as he moved from place to place.
They represent a glimpse into a living tradition of open-air
preaching, necessarily improvised and reworked over time,
according to the mood of the crowd or the specific challenges
of the occasion.

What is clear, however, is that parables are illustrative
both of Jesus' oratorical technique and of his way of
doing theology. He uses comparison and metaphor—
"midrashically"—to open a door into a bigger reality. In his
parables, Jesus shows us what the things of God are *like* and
how one understanding of God may be *likened to* another
in order to expand our mental horizons. He juxtaposes and
contrasts very different things so as to make unexpected and
startling connections that broaden our perspectives. These
are the new "gestalts" we discussed in the previous chapter.
And, indeed, when asked questions, Jesus tells stories that

connect with the narrative of our own lives and cajole us to use our imaginations to think and respond for ourselves. He refuses to offer single, closed interpretations, and constantly instructs his listeners to come to their own conclusions: "'Let anyone with ears to hear listen!'" (Mk 4:9, 4:23; Mt 11:15, 13:9, 13:43; Lk 8:8, 14:35).

How disturbing this must have been for those religious professionals who made a living offering definitive legal verdicts and fixed moral rulings, or those leaders concerned to ensure conformity to established norms and practices. Throughout the gospels, Jesus offers the possibility of multiple alternative connections and interpretations, and encourages ordinary people to engage with the business of working out their own understandings of who God is for them, and of the demands God makes on their—and now our—spiritual and religious lives.

While this was once judged to be such profound and blasphemous subversion, today the church admires Jesus for it! We preach and teach about what he did: how he held the crowds spellbound, communicated important truths in everyday language, drew people to himself, and offered them and their communities the possibility of transformation.

Might the same disciplines of imagination still work for us today?

Re-Imagination and the Freeing of the Church

Imagine, if you will, the possibility of a church congregation encouraged to think imaginatively; where sermons and teaching programs are not apprehensive about the possibility of people thinking for themselves, even if this means there is a variety of (occasionally eccentric) theological worldviews and opinions within the community. Imagine, instead, that in this congregation sermons and

theological teaching are deliberately designed to invite
or allow people to question, explore, and make creative
connections with the unexpected and the novel; rather than
offer or reinforce merely predictable, time-worn, and clichéd
solutions. Imagine a Christian community where questions
such as "What if?", "Could you ever imagine?", and "What
do you think?" are routinely part of sermons, discussions, and
informal conversations, and a normal expectation of Christian
discipleship.

It can take a little time for a congregation to come to
think like this, to gain the confidence to find the exercise
not too uncomfortable. My own experience of leading such
congregations suggests it takes about a year for most people
to engage with such a novel methodology; though, of course,
some people never manage it. But during this time they come
to discover that their "little faith," as they so often describe it,
might in reality be significant and worth contributing to the
common quest for shared wisdom!

Such an approach is able to "lift" a congregation and
create a sense of coherence and mutual involvement,
accountability, and purposefulness. Using sermons, Scripture
study, group work, short courses, and pastoral encounters
to encourage the congregation to "use their ears to hear,"
think laterally, and believe in their own capacity to create
alternative and trustworthy interpretations, does actually *raise
expectations*. People begin to apply this approach to issues in
their daily discipleship and living. It encourages them to be
more resourceful and effective, enabling them to turn what
might once have been seen as the "dire threat of change"
into welcome opportunities for growth. It empowers people,
bringing an ever more confident thoughtfulness and creative
energy to their personal and communal Christian journey
and ministry. It offers the very real possibility of fundamental
congregational transformation.

Significantly too, it has the capacity to turn fearfulness—fear of failure, fear of bad decisions, fear of outsiders, and fear of newness—into opportunities for "grace-full" self-discovery and flourishing. It enables us to break through horizons limited artificially by our fear and by the barriers we have erected for our self-preservation. Using our imaginations creatively is ultimately all about healing and wholeness—*shalom-making*—as a robust and life-giving connection or synergy is made between how people experience God and how they understand God. As we use our imaginations to recognize and appreciate multiple and different perspectives from our own, we experience the erosion of the insider-outsider, us-and-them, mentality that has blighted the church for far too long. Using our imaginations empowers us to move beyond the limits of what we have always believed is possible, and that has so constrained us in the past. It transforms stunted and impoverished vision into real human flourishing and a desire to connect with the wider world beyond.

On Reconnecting

Reconnecting with the Universe

Flowing from this call to engage our imaginative capacities to promote human flourishing is the second task which awaits the Christian community: the need for us to reconnect with the universe that is our home.

In recent decades it has become evident that we have very largely lost our connection with the universe and the natural world of which we are a part. For those of us living in urban or suburban environments—and this is now the majority of the world's population—this is literally the case. Living in built-up or high rise communities, not only do we largely lose any visible sense of inhabiting a landscape, but also light pollution almost totally prevents us from catching a glimpse of the majestic and awe-inspiring vastness of the night skies above our heads.

This loss of the awareness of being physically part of a landscape and the invisibility of the horizons means we have also lost touch with our psychological and spiritual relationship to the universe. We have forgotten that we ourselves are literally star dust: full of atoms and precious minerals that go back to the dawn of time. Consequently, if we do manage to glimpse the starry sky, we no longer think of it as our original home and birthplace. If we feel anything at all, we feel mostly only fear: fear of our smallness before its vastness; fear of what we don't understand and can't control; fear of the spontaneity of nature over the predictability of technology; fear of the unknown and of the future; fear of the apparently empty blackness that alerts us to feelings we may prefer not to articulate; and fear of our annihilation or alienation by some as-yet-unarticulated dread or unknown force.

We have lost our connection to the sheer breathtaking magic of the universe we live in. Our ability to respond with wonder, awe, and gratitude has been dulled by a now habitual, almost pornographic gaze whereby, because we cannot purchase and consume what we see, we choose to disparage, devalue, and—ultimately—simply ignore it. Yet how possible it is that reconnection with our universe, and with the natural world around us, could lead to a healing of our hunger and our *dis*-ease! How possible it is that regaining a sense of being part of an astonishing and intricate wholeness could enable us to regain a sense of integrity and belonging, and so help us to flourish as a community!

How might our Christian communities help encourage this reconnection?

Spirituality as a Tool for Reconnection

Today's Christians need to be encouraged to explore our spiritual resources; for we have vast treasures to share, even if much of it may need imaginative re-translation for use in our world. Sadly, there is little sense among Jesus' disciples that we are being called to explore how our own spiritual practices and disciplines might facilitate this reconnection. There is even less sign that the church is seeking to go out and engage with the spiritual needs of non-attendees or, just as crucially, to learn from them the ways in which they explore these issues for themselves.

Even if, for a moment, we were to take the superficial view that much of what passes for spiritual practice in the wider community (often denigrated as a "pick and choose" or "DIY" approach) is unfocused, self-centered, or self-indulgent, it is *not automatically the case* that what results is necessarily always any less life-giving than some of what passes for spiritual practice in our religious institutions.

What's important, instead, is to step outside and make the connections, have the conversations, build the relationships, and see what happens next. In this way the church might just be freed into a more effective and life-enhancing ministry. Exploration of the breadth and depth of different forms of spirituality and spiritual practice is not only liberative for those who engage in it, but an urgent means of dialogue and mission.

Making the Darkness Visible

A first step in reconnecting with the natural world and the universe is to make its invisibility—its hiddenness or darkness—visible to us; to make it present to our consciousness, and then to become *comfortable* in it. We have forgotten that we have as much primary connection with the universe as with the mothers who bore us. We have lost sight—literally—of the fact that the universe is *full* of things, not least the myriad galaxies, stars, and planets, the almost undetectable "stuff" scientists identify as "dark matter," as well as the ever-expanding frontiers of the cosmos itself. We no longer recognize the beauty and majesty of it all.

We need to allow the potent mystery of the universe that beckons us to begin to play upon our souls, so that we can rediscover our primary home and the sacred space that is both the start and end point of our spiritual journey. We need to cultivate the sense that our connection to the universe, and with the natural world, makes mystics of us all. And by "mystic" I don't mean someone with access to arcane knowledge that involves a turning away from the world, but rather someone whose gaze is fully on the world in a way that allows them to see its beauty and value. Someone able to make the *connections between* that beauty and value, and the need for global justice and the flourishing of *all creation.* We need to develop ways of helping people create personal and shared spiritualities that *root them in the earth*, in habits of "care-full-ness" for its peoples, eco-systems, and the inter-relatedness of species and planet; while at the same time drawing people into deep familiarity with what lies beyond and around us.

When Space Becomes Place

Becoming *at-ease* in this way will involve us in exploring how we occupy and transform space. We will examine how "space" becomes "place," by *inscribing* "space" with meaning and so transforming it into "place" with memories, stories, meanings, relationships, and values.

Imagine, for instance, moving into a new house in a new neighborhood. The house becomes a home when we fill it with treasured objects, personal belongings, and—more especially—with the deep familiarity of personal routines.

We work to create a home that is both ordinary and also extraordinary: safe, secure, and at the same time special, hallowed, and sacred. Similarly the location of our home becomes neighborhood and community for us when we move about in it, get to know people, and make connections. Places are spaces full of human "rootedness," belonging, history, association, and story. In this way we make relationships and networks beyond the home and into the wider community and world.

Aboriginal Australian people have done this in a particular way to articulate and transmit their sense of being at home within a landscape that is their sacred homeland as much as their physical dwelling place. They have created invisible threads of connection in the form of memorized and cherished stories, or "songlines," transmitted down the generations, that then become "visible"—remembered and retold—as the people move through the landscape. Songs and stories about their origins in the archetypal Dream Time—in what (as we saw in the previous chapter) we might call the time before the Big Bang—when all of creation was still in darkness in the "mind of God."

This idea of "song lines" has much to teach us, as Sandercock explores in *Cosmopolis II* (2003, 227-228). For while people have always located themselves in their own physical environments in similar ways—by creating sacred landscapes, holy sites, pilgrimages, and gathering places with their associated sagas, legends, and stories— there is much to be said for Christian communities trying to create and share similar narrative experiences and journeys in our own neighborhoods. For in every community—even those at the heart of our urban and suburban neighborhoods—there is the potential to identify sites full of association, story, and meaning, by creating lines of memory, connection, and celebration.

Embracing the Fullness of Time

The English poet Philip Larkin memorably speaks of how "Days are where we live. / They come, they wake us / Time and time over" (*Collected Poems*, 2003, 98). Yet how our days all too often slip by unappreciated, unnoticed, and unmarked. Thus, when they run short and death approaches, we often find ourselves unable to function or make sense of our experience.

A way of urgent reconnection with our mortality lies in appreciating the difference between calendar time—the most obvious reading of the "days" of Larkin's lines—and those one-off life events of great significance. Too often we live our workaday lives in a blur of hasty "unrecognition"—"thin time"—as we rush eagerly towards the next moment we consider important: a day off, family celebration, vacation, or a public or religious festival. But it is precisely in learning to fully appreciate and celebrate the *richness* of such "thick time," "magic moments," or never-to-be-repeated events when life is *felt* to be different, that we might come to transform our ordinary daily living. For each moment of every day can, if we choose, become instants and occasions when time seems to stand still and doorways open into greater perceptions of reality.

Developing a heightened sense of awareness of the contrasting "thinness and thickness" of reality in this way allows us to see the world, and to value life, differently. Here the Jewish notion of Sabbath speaks powerfully of our need to embrace the fullness of time. Sabbath is about much more than having a restful day off after a hard week's work.

Sabbath—"*shavath*"—recalls God desisting from *creating* on the seventh day. It describes a time dedicated to simply savoring and delighting in what has been created; enjoying "what is." (Importantly, it means *not creating*, rather than *not working,* as is often assumed. So, for example, writing on the Sabbath is forbidden, but reading is not.) Sabbath, as Walter Brueggemann remarks somewhere, is "a new way of ordering the world." And "Sabbath living" is about trying to incorporate in our own lives Jesus' encouragement: "not [to] worry about your life, what you will eat or what you will drink, or about your body," (Mt 6:25), and his suggestion to "look at the birds of the air" (6:26), and recognize that "worrying [will not] add a single hour to your span of life" (6:27).

Practicing "Sabbath living," discovering, embracing, and sharing the wholeness and fullness of God's peace-giving "shalom," is one way in which we might empower people to live out the fullness of our humanity, and to explore the things that give meaning and value to our experience of being alive. But, though not all Christians and Christian communities have managed this task, it is clear that promoting such an adventure in the wider community is an urgent creative dimension to any risk-filled ministry.

On Re-Enchanting

Rediscovering the Magic of Living

The interest these days in all things magical may, with some confidence, be seen as a response to the feeling, increasingly expressed by many, that life itself has "lost its magic." The more we become dependent on machines that would themselves once have appeared magical—not least the burgeoning of forms of artificial intelligence and instantaneous global communications systems—the more we discover that a sense of the *original* magic and mystery of creation is being progressively obscured. Consequently, there is a tangible thirst for anything and everything that might offer some route (and ideally a shortcut!) to regaining a sense of re-enchantment.

The word "enchantment" inevitably conjures up ideas about the "magical": "casting spells" and being "bewitched," and "charmed," or else of becoming "enthralled" or "captivated" by some (usually quixotic or malevolent) power. For many people, such ideas are to be regarded with suspicion: the very antithesis of all that is "godly and good." It is no doubt true, on one level, that a revival of "magical thinking" has accompanied the development of ideas about "a God of one's own." (See Beck, 87, 125-132.) But to take this view over-simplistically is to fall into the trap of reducing the vast mystery of the universe into some act of mere slight of hand or muttered incantation. It is tantamount to narrowing the sphere of God's self-revelation to the words of Scripture alone (as happened at the time of the Protestant Reformation); instead of seeing the whole created universe as expressing the mystery and majesty of God. For there is, indeed, real magic and mystery all around us, if we care to acknowledge and celebrate it.

The Sacredness of Life

In response to this urge for re-enchantment, Mary Grey (*Sacred Longings*, 2003) talks powerfully about the need to create a "sacramental poetics":

> A sacramental poetics is about … the transformation of everyday perception and experience into something that satisfies the deepest longings. … [It] appeals to the imagination: by appealing to the basic realities in our lives, bread, water, oil, salt, earth, trees, in word and symbol, prayer and gesture, it awakens a depth dimension and an experience of the sacred. … [It] has the power to re-enchant a broken-hearted world, speaking the language and the music of the heart … (86).

Such a "sacramental poetics" (with "poetics" coming from the Greek notion of "*poiesis*": words that have *real transformative impact*) encourages openness to fresh perceptions of reality, of everyday things, and of the "mundane," openness to what Grey goes on to call the "creative potential of chaos" (95). This suggestion of cultivating an awareness of, and response to, the poetic or creative potential within "chaos"—to "that which is still to emerge, or come into being or focus"—sketches out a very clear and urgent invitation for the Christian community to be at the forefront of efforts to rearticulate the sacredness, the "magic," at the heart of creation.

This clearly legitimizes—should that still be needed—the church's passionate involvement in a broad range of "green" and "eco-justice" issues: care of the environment, sustainability of natural resources, animal rights, the formation of a radically creation-friendly ethics, and so on. The revaluation of the unique significance of the world as "a onetime project" (Berry, *The Sacred Universe*, 2009, 175), and the re-experiencing of its deep mystery, is gradually beginning to have a creative and transformative impact in many parts of the church; particularly, through the involvement of individual Christians in secular interest groups and initiatives.

But ideas about "sacramental poetics" and creative potential also point to an equally urgent agenda for Christian communities everywhere. For if the task of re-enchantment applies to the sacredness of the planet and to the life it sustains, then it applies equally to people.

Transformation of the Self

Much of what we have explored thus far has already pointed us in this direction. Jesus' parabolic teaching (and its enactment in his healing ministry) is an invitation to broken-hearted individuals and fractured communities of people to reconsider how we belong within the "*shalom*"—the kingdom-kindom—of God. This in turn can, as we have seen, be translated into more contemporary ideas about new gestalts and communities of transformation.

Grey's notion of "sacramental poetics" is also an invitation—indeed a mandate—to re-experience "the self in a more complete sense" (Edgar, *Guide to Imagework*, 2004, 101). It is an opportunity to rediscover ourselves as "magical" and "enchanted" or, if we prefer, as "sacred" and "made in God's image." It is an occasion for seeing how, in our own physical bodies and enfleshed souls, we might "reshape the boundaries of consciousness" (Edgar, 112) in order to see ourselves afresh. We see ourselves, not just as sinful, fallen—or even as "still-imperfect"—creatures, but as beings caught up in a God-inspired vocational process of becoming, in a movement towards *shalom-salaam*, wholeness, and (as we'll explore in the following chapter) greater personhood.

So if Christian communities are to help us rediscover ourselves as sons and daughters of the one creator God, or indeed as "sacred selves awaiting re-enchantment," then we need to commit ourselves to a hands-on ministry of conversation, exploration, discernment, empowerment, sharing, and celebration. The process of rediscovering and re-experiencing our embodied selves as truly enchanted or "God-spelled"—as the site of a "sacramental poetics" of our own—works on several important levels and requires us to be actively involved in several distinct forms of spiritual exercise. Each of these is interconnected because each is an aspect of the one question of desire. As I suggested earlier, a significant role for the church lies in its becoming fluent in understanding and using the language of desire. The reality of desire—as an intellectual idea *and* as a physical emotion (and which is it mostly for us?), as well as being the meeting place of the human and divine—is one that demands urgent and creative attention. Indeed, it holds the key to re-learning those "Three R's" of re-imagination, reconnection, and re-enchantment.

A Hands-on Ministry of Transformation

This process of rediscovery or re-experiencing needs to address, in no particular order, a four-fold movement: from the pornographic to the erotic; from intimacy to community; from falseness to authenticity; and from consumption to celebration. My suggestion is that a truly effective risk-shaped ministry—the spiritual exercises and disciplines it practices and the care-giving it offers—must involve itself in promoting wholeness and greater personhood in each of these areas in turn.

In terms of the *movement from the pornographic to the erotic*, the idea of a "sacramental poetics" demands a frank acknowledgement about the ways in which, on the one hand, we have allowed ourselves to become passive voyeurs and not active participants in life; and on the other hand, the manner in which we have come to divorce the erotic from the creative and reduce it to what is almost entirely associated with the genital and sexually explicit. We have devalued our understanding of our physical self-image and personal identity to the level of what is entirely shallow and external: our physical appearance and dress. We have allowed much human interaction to become superficial, one-dimensional, and disengaged. Witness our still instinctive retreat into self-absorption and self-protection, rather than responding positively to global need. We have failed to demonstrate that the erotic is primarily and intimately bound up with what is creative, healing, and life-giving.

In a similar fashion, the *movement from intimacy to community* requires us to de-center our fixation with seeking to prioritize and satisfy only those things that affect us as individuals, whether in fulfilling our personal desires or achieving the guarantee of personal salvation. We need to learn, instead, to shift our self-understanding away from the idea that we are purely and definitively isolated individuals (or closed families or nations), in order to embrace the bigger reality that "God-shaped" personhood is ultimately about being persons-in-community, or in global interconnectedness. Real human intimacy finds more resonance, and indeed offers greater fulfillment and impact, when it is created and shared—"intimated"—among other persons. Such a "community of intimacy" is not a banal contradiction, but the working out and reshaping of the human urge for self-realization on a broader canvas and to a different tune.

The *movement from falseness to authenticity* strikes at the heart of our sense of who we think we are. Falseness—like its cognate "falsehood," the medieval English crime of wearing the wrong hat in public and so assuming a false identity—suggests that we are complicit in an act of delusion: the delusion of our selves as much, if not more, than of those around us. While we may understand this falseness as ultimately "not our fault" (and blame instead our mythical forebears in Eden), as fundamentally existential (where to be human is to be essentially imperfect), or as something non-problematic, meaningless, and easily ignored, the call to wake up to the realization that we might be other than we are, has always resonated deeply with the experience of people down the centuries and across all cultures. There appears to be something within our hard-wiring that calls us to strive towards authenticity, and towards the astonishingly simple discovery that our authentic personal and collective striving to change who we are—and become instead whatever it is we might yet be—is central to the flourishing of all humanity.

Finally, the *movement from consumption to celebration* involves us in a recognition of the eternal hunger that afflicts us as a species. While for far too many people the issue of hunger is a frighteningly urgent problem of daily existence from which the rest of us cannot in all conscience turn our faces, there is a manifest sense in which hunger is also a profoundly, and no less fundamental, spiritual condition. We are driven by a deep need to take, possess, devour, and consume: anything and everything, food, possessions, experience, money, fame, affirmation; in search of an ultimately elusive security. We are forever unable to find satisfaction. We are never sated and always left longing for more. How, then, might we be ever moved to celebration?

All too frequently, however, the very idea of celebration is itself the product of our consumerist mentality. Celebration requires things to consume, forms of entertainment or amusement to fill the void created by our need for intimacy, and a desire for fairly instant gratification. Celebration of our human identity and condition—and of the manifold and various ways in which it might be understood: not least through religious story or secular scientific narrative—is, however, all too often singularly lacking in contemporary western society. It is as though we have forgotten what real celebration is, and how to do it. Consequently, a "sacramental poetical" approach to celebration will be one that seeks to honor the whole breadth, depth, and height of the human condition: its givenness, limitations, persistent tendency to hubris and tragedy, and its ultimate potential.

Arousing the Human Being

What Jesus does time and again throughout his earthly ministry is to "arouse the Human Being" (Wink, 2002, 80) in people. He makes the connection between the core of his own being and that of others. If this "arousing the Human Being in each other" were part of a risk-shaped ministry, it would allow the creation of a spark of aliveness in wounded and needy people that might then just flare up and cause the transformation of our fractured and beleaguered communities. It would allow us to discover more than we had any right to expect or hope for: the transformative re-imagining of the way things have always been presented to us, a reconnection with a prophetic but pragmatic vision for an inclusive kingdom-kindom of God, and the dramatic and astounding rediscovery of our being caught up and drawn ever deeper into the enchanting and re-enchanting wholeness of God.

I, for one, believe that it is not too late for Christian communities to be caught up in that same process of enchanting wholeness, and that this task might legitimately become part of the church's ministry.

Time to explore!

Here are some ideas for you to discuss with friends in your local church or community:

- Can you imagine a church where pastoral ministry is geared to nurturing the imagination? What impact would this have on your church?

- What difference could be made by a more radically imaginative approach to the way things are run in your local community?

Time for some action!

Here are some suggestions for you to try out:

- Try out the "song lines" idea in your local community. First list those places where people gather: play-grounds for toddlers and parents; street corners or outside particular stores for teenagers; shopping malls for families; under archways for the homeless, and so on; as well as sites where disaster and tragedy have occurred.

Next, sketch the natural and historic features (contours, valleys, hills, streams, battle grounds, and monuments) on a map. Let each group identify the sites they particularly "inhabit," and the stories of their lives and activities that turn these spaces into places. As each group speaks, let them be heard by the others, recorded in some way, and then included on the map.

Then link these sites together to make a community chart that turns these song lines into a living document, as people from many different backgrounds and generations cooperate to create and explore their mutual rootedness and connection, and a sense of their diverse but shared human history and identity. Finally, find some way of celebrating this within the wider community.

- What difference to your community might be made by celebrating the "magic" of life?

For church leaders:

- In what ways have you raised expectations among your congregation? What have been the obstacles to this work?

- In what ways do you consider your ministry to be about arousing the "Human Being" in people?

- What would a more intentionally transformative approach to your preaching, teaching, and community life look like?

Be Friending

Part 1: A Community of Resurrected Humanity

Cards on the Table

It is no small matter to suggest that, after two thousand years of its history, the real task of church remains that of encouraging communities to "re-experienc[e] the self in a more complete sense" (Edgar, 2004, 101) and of exploring with those outside the church how humanity is "God-spelled." It is no small matter that we are still struggling to truly discover ourselves as "sacred selves" awaiting re-enchantment, to understand what it really means to be sons and daughters of God, and then be confidently able to live out this knowledge in our daily lives.

It is no small matter because—despite the death and resurrection of Jesus and the pouring out of the Spirit on all flesh—there is still a deep ambivalence within the Christian community that manifests in the way that it habitually prefers to see itself as *fundamentally set apart* from that which is "of the world." In order to *theologically* justify its existence, the Christian community feels the need to be "redeemed from" God's creation; and consequently, it cannot quite believe that the world is good, blessed by, and full of, the ever-creative presence of God. Because of a deep-seated *theological* association between sin, "fallen" humanity, and the world, the Christian community itself has stumbled into the trap of equating this "fallen" state with the nature of creation itself, and so has forgotten that the universe is our sacred home, a welcoming and *friendly* place. More remarkably, it is no small matter because the Christian community appears unable to recognize that, precisely *because redemption has taken place,* there is now a different sort of mission and ministry for it to undertake.

This historic ambivalence towards the world (famously reflected in Rom 12:2 and 1 Jn 2:15) and to the idea that, as the body of God, the universe is "God-spelled," is inevitably reflected in the way we understand, approach, and encounter God. While God is routinely *believed* to be "all good," what still characterizes much everyday Christian discourse and practice appears to be rooted in a deep, generally unarticulated, and often spiritually destructive ambivalence towards God, that sometimes even manifests in a downright fearful paranoia. While this is certainly not unique to the Christian faith, there is clear scriptural witness to this ambivalence.

The question then becomes how a risk-shaped ministry might help people engage with this ambivalence and perhaps develop a more wholesome understanding of God.

Understanding Ambivalence

Ambivalence about God exists throughout the Scriptures, but perhaps most memorably when we read in the Torah how "the Lord used to speak to Moses face to face, as one speaks to a friend" (Ex 33:11). We also hear God say "no one shall see me and live" (Ex 33:20). Is God then a friend or an enemy? Dare we look on the face of God? Will we live—or die?

The Hebrew Scriptures mention the "face" of God on around 2100 occasions (Basset, *Holy Anger,* 2007, 170). Frequently, we read of people praying that God's face might not be hidden or turned away:

> But I, O Lord, cry out to you;
>> in the morning my prayer comes before you.
> O Lord, why do you cast me off?
>> Why do you hide your face from me? (Ps 88:13-
>> 14).

They pray that it might, rather, be turned towards them in blessing:

> The Lord bless you and keep you;
>> the Lord make his face to shine upon you, and be
>> gracious to you;
>> the Lord lift up his countenance upon you, and give
>> you peace (Num 6:24-26).

However, closer scrutiny of the texts suggests that God's face is turned away *when God feels provoked* to anger by humanity, that God is not vindictive, but ever concerned for the wellbeing of humanity, that God would rather be deprived of "face to face" intimacy than risk human welfare; even though, when this happens, both God and humanity are losers.

The point is well illustrated by the story of Jacob wrestling with God at the ford of Jabbok. (The inspiration for what follows here is Basset, *Holy Anger*, 2007, *passim*.) This revealing episode is part of the narrative of Jacob's return to his homeland after an absence of many years and his approach to his estranged brother Esau (Gen 32 and 33).

Jacob is not sure of how Esau will react and so sends servants ahead with presents to appease him, instructing them to say: "'I have oxen, donkeys, flocks, male and female slaves; and I have sent to tell my lord, in order that I may find favor in your sight'" (Gen 32:5). When the messengers return with word that Esau himself is coming to meet him, Jacob is terrified. He divides all his people and property into two groups "thinking, 'If Esau comes to one company and destroys it, then the company that is left will escape'" (8).

He prays to God: "'O God of my father Abraham and God of my father Isaac, *O Lord who said to me*, "Return to your country and to your kindred, and I will do you good"'"(9, my emphasis). And: "'Deliver me, please, from the hand of my brother, from the hand of Esau, for I am afraid of him; he may come and kill us all …. *Yet you have said*, "I will surely do you good, and make your offspring as the sand of the sea, which cannot be counted because of their number"'"" (11-12, my emphasis). He then attempts to further appease Esau with successive waves of gifts, each spaced out to maximize the effect and ensure the earliest possible warning of danger: "For he thought, 'I may appease him with the present that goes ahead of me, and afterwards I shall see his face; perhaps he will accept me'" (20).

That night he sleeps by the ford of Jabbok and a curious dream reveals his anxiety.

> Jacob was left alone; and a man wrestled with him until daybreak. When the man saw that he did not prevail against Jacob, he struck him on the hip socket; and Jacob's hip was put out of joint as he wrestled with him. Then he said, "Let me go, for the day is breaking." But Jacob said, "I will not let you go, unless you bless me." So he said to him, "What is your name?" And he said, "Jacob." Then the man said, "You shall no longer be called Jacob, but Israel, for you have striven with God and with humans, and have prevailed." Then Jacob asked him, "Please tell me your name." But he said, "Why is it that you ask my name?" And there he blessed him. So Jacob called the place Peniel, saying, "For I have seen God face to face, and yet my life is preserved" (32: 24-30).

Next day, when he discovers Esau arriving with four hundred men, Jacob prepares for the worst. He approaches Esau "bowing himself to the ground seven times" (33:3). To Jacob's relief Esau welcomes Jacob warmly, but then asks:

> "What do you mean by all this company that I met?" Jacob answered, "To find favor with my lord." But Esau said, "I have enough, my brother; keep what you have for yourself." Jacob said, "No, please; if I find favor with you, then accept my present from my hand; *for truly to see your face is like seeing the face of God*— since you have received me with such favour" (8-10, my emphasis).

The story of the encounter between Jacob and Esau serves as a foil for that between God and Jacob. In the former, Jacob assumes a negative, indeed, violent, response from his brother and takes appropriate precautions to preserve his life. In the event, he is proved wrong: Esau is pleased to see him. Hence Jacob's comment that, seeing Esau's face *"is like seeing the face of God"* (10): it is as likely to bring destruction as a blessing.

In a similar fashion, in the dream encounter, Jacob cannot tell if his attacker is an evil demon or not; he cannot see his assailant's face. He assumes the man with whom he wrestles is an adversary. But he is wrong. It seems that, in coming to Jabbok, God intends to bless Jacob with an intimate face to face encounter in his hour of need. But God's approach is *misunderstood* by Jacob in his anxiety about his own meeting with his brother, and so a struggle takes place. Eventually at dawn, however, Jacob sees God face to face and his "life is preserved" (Gen 32:30). He receives the blessing of being renamed Israel for that "struggle with God."

Pondering the Source of Ambivalence

Just as we may never fully know someone's feelings and respond appropriately until we have actually seen their face—largely a process of subconscious recognition—so we need to learn that we can either keep God at arm's length, wanting unambiguous certainty before approaching, as Jacob tried to do with Esau, or else we can recognize that God's approach to us is ever imminent; ever ready and waiting to happen. God always seeks the intimacy of an encounter with us. And, as we read in the story we call the prodigal son—a text which is very much the New Testament equivalent to that of Jacob and Esau—God is forever watching and waiting to run towards us and embrace us (Lk 15:11-32).

This ambivalence is, of course, a matter of record. It is there in the Scriptures as the "word of God" and it points to the distinct possibility that Scripture reveals at least as much about the history of human insecurity and prejudice, and of our own ambivalence about the "otherness" of God, as it does about the development of God's relationship with humanity. If we are not to be forever fearfully fleeing God's presence, like Jacob and the prodigal son, then we need to risk trusting God as much as God risks being misunderstood and rejected by us.

So how are we to react when we encounter the presence of God? Will our face be hardened with fear or anger that might cause God to turn away? Or do we welcome God with a smile that will be mirrored in God's own face? For, as the story of Esau, Jacob, and the Jabbok encounter reveals, the disturbing truth is that God lets us decide whether to choose to cast God as a dangerous and uninvited stranger or as a welcome friend. God will not impose a response on us but is content, instead, to wait for a time when we can *step outside* the limits of our "fear-full" ambivalence and, instead, be embraced by God on terms of healing intimacy. This, as we saw earlier, is what Etty Hillesum discovered.

From Ambivalence to Commitment

This ambivalence about God and about the world begs the question of what sort of ministry is demanded of the community of resurrected humanity that the church is meant to be. What sort of ministry might help people overcome this ambivalence and commit to risking a "face to face" engagement with God—"divinity"—and with the world?

Throughout the Hebrew Scriptures there is clear witness to the unfolding of the relationship between God and humanity—and of humanity's growing understanding of God. Again, this development belies the simplistic distinction many of us hold between the God of the "Old" and "New" Testaments, whereby the older "barbaric and merciless" divinity is superseded by the God "revealed in Jesus."

An illustration of this shift in human understanding of God is especially visible in the book we call "Isaiah." Mainstream scholarship understands Isaiah to be a work of several generations and authored by several hands, from the mid eighth century BCE onwards. In its earliest phase ("First Isaiah") God is presented as a cultic God, one who is entirely bound up with the survival of Israel over the other nations and their gods. This exclusive theological view shifts in "Second Isaiah" to present God as not only concerned for Jerusalem, but for the entire earth over which the God of Israel is now understood to reign. Finally, "Third Isaiah" roots this cosmic vision of God's sovereignty in God's practical commitment to inclusive justice, compassion, and neighborliness that is memorably articulated in the vision of Isaiah 61:1-3a:

> The spirit of the Lord God is upon me,
>> because the Lord has anointed me;
> he has sent me to bring good news to the oppressed,
>> to bind up the broken-hearted,
> to proclaim liberty to the captives,
>> and release to the prisoners;
> to proclaim the year of the Lord's favor,
>> and the day of vengeance of our God;
>> to comfort all who mourn;
> to provide for those who mourn in Zion—
>> to give them a garland instead of ashes,
> the oil of gladness instead of mourning,
>> the mantle of praise instead of a faint spirit.

It is, of course, this text that is later reiterated in Luke 4:18-19, and which provides that gospel with the interpretative key to Jesus' earthly ministry. For wherever Jesus goes he seeks to "bring good news to the oppressed" through the performance of a practical ministry of liberation, healing, and restoration.

What is remarkable about Jesus is his complete lack of ambivalence. This is evident not only in his sense of a positive filial identity with God—he sees God as his father, "*abba*"—but also in his consistent use of the language of friendship. Jesus fully embodies the shift from ambivalence to a deeply relational commitment both to God and to all the people he encounters in his ministry. And this, in turn, allows him to inhabit a place beyond ambivalence and beyond suspicion, envy, and fear: a place of radical and inclusive friendship.

I Call You Friends

It is not unusual, of course, to see Jesus addressing strangers as friends: "'I tell you, my friends'" (Lk 12:4), "'Friend, your sins are forgiven you'" (Lk 5:20), "'Friend, I am doing you no wrong'" (Mt 20:13; see also Mt 22:12; 26:50). And while we have no way of knowing whether his practice was unusual or not, Jesus does appear to have a particular appreciation of friendship that transcends any utilitarian understanding.

In John's account of the Last Supper, Jesus famously takes a towel and washes his disciples' feet. Though they routinely called him "rabbi," "lord," or "master," he performs for them the duty normally allotted to a household servant. This acting out the reversal of normative social roles speaks of his transcendence of the master-slave dynamic that then *allows them all* to step out into a new place of friendship, openness, and intimacy:

> "No one has greater love than this, to lay down one's life for one's friends. You are my friends if you do what I command you. I do not call you servants any longer, because the servant does not know what the master is doing; but I have called you friends, because I have made known to you everything that I have heard from my Father" (Jn 15:13-15).

It is clear, too, from this incident that friendship with Jesus is not a privileged or exclusive relationship. It comes at a cost to those who choose it: "You are my friends *if* you do what I command you;" and "I have called you friends, *because* I have made known to you everything ...." Friendship with Jesus is a vigorous call to creative relationality. Friendship with Jesus is ever to be *actively* lived out in the generative and healing love that flows, runs over, and spreads among friends and strangers and out into neighborhoods and nations.

Do You Love Me?

The magnitude of this movement beyond personal friendship into the realm of justice for the wider community may be reflected in the epilogue to John's Gospel, which almost certainly was a later addition by another hand, and reflects the situation of the church at that time:

> When they had finished breakfast, Jesus said to Simon Peter, "Simon son of John, do you love me more than these?" He said to him, "Yes, Lord; you know that I love you." Jesus said to him, "Feed my lambs." A second time he said to him, "Simon son of John, do you love me?" He said to him, "Yes, Lord; you know that I love you." Jesus said to him, "Tend my sheep." He said to him the third time, "Simon son of John, do you love me?" Peter felt hurt because he said to him the third time, "Do you love me?" And he said to him, "Lord, you know everything; you know that I love you." Jesus said to him, "Feed my sheep" (Jn 21:15-17).

The word "love" in Jesus' first question to Peter—"*agapao*"—suggests not only fondness between friends, but came quickly to epitomize the self-forgetful, self-sacrificing love of Christ for the world. Jesus seems here to ask Peter outright whether he has this kind of love. But Peter responds with a less strong synonym—"*phileo*"—that lacks the social dimension.

This depiction of Peter's inability to love as Jesus intends is redolent of the undoubted tensions within the persecuted Christian community at the end of the first century that was struggling to live out the radical teachings of Jesus in a dangerous world. It is redolent, too, of today's Christian communities that are constrained, on the one hand, by the deadening weight of bureaucracy and tradition and, on the other hand, by the reality of dwindling numbers, a lack of vision and energy, and the sheer riskiness of trying to reach out and engage with a world that no longer speaks the same language.

Moving from Image to Likeness

Time and again Jesus shows us how we are called to live among other people without ambivalence. He embodies what McIntosh calls "a pattern of relationships not founded on fear and envy but resourced by the endless generosity of God" (McIntosh, *Divine Teaching*, 2008, 101). And he sees Jesus as encouraging us, at every step, to "risk the full calling of [our] creaturely life" (180).

Our lived response to this "full calling" is one that requires us not to limit ourselves to hiding behind the *image* of Jesus as risk-taker, but rather to *put on his likeness*: to become the embodied and unambivalent friendship of Jesus in action, and risk-takers after his example. We are to imitate him in obedience to his persistent challenge to "go and do likewise," and so—with the Spirit's guidance—help usher in a new habit of creative friendship-making that woos, attracts, and inspires all who encounter it. Not "a slavish imitation [of Jesus] but ... the freedom to respond ... in accord with our own ... integrity" (Primavesi, *Sacred Gaia*, 2000, 114-115) and as befits our own very different world.

Jesus performed many unambivalent acts of healing and transformative friendship, but it is evident to us now that they were but tokens of a much greater movement towards human wholeness. As we have seen, Walter Wink characterizes this ministry—of such cosmic proportions—as one of "arousing the Human Being" (2002, *passim*) in all people, while Swinton talks of Jesus' ability to "resurrect the person" (2000, *passim*), and enable people to discover themselves to be "loved by God beyond all measure and created in God's image for loving fellowship ..." (9). This discovery moves us "beyond our socially bound expectations" (51) to create "friendships [that] are both *centripetal* and *centrifugal*, reaching inward to contribute to the building of a loving and inclusive community, and outward to embrace and stand with the 'outsiders'" (51).

And as we dare ourselves to imitate these transformative acts, we too must ever seek to offer each other what Brueggemann calls the "empowerment and summons that generates human possibility" (Brueggemann, *Redescribing Reality*, 2009, 134).

Go Home to Your Friends

The story of Jesus' healing of the "Gerasene demoniac" (Mk 5:1-20) ends with him telling the man, now restored to his senses, to "Go home to your friends" (Mk 5:19). And, indeed, he went back to his friends in the Decapolis and told them all he had encountered. But where is our home and who are our friends?

It may be that the home and the friends to whom we also are bidden to return are to be found in the church. But the church can only be a true community of friendship "when it reveals inclusive love, and … realizes the limitations of its human-made boundaries and strives to build a space for love …" (Willows and Swinton, 2002, 103). It has not always lived up to that calling.

Love and friendship are the healing gifts God offers to the community. But they are gifts that flow less from concern with the details of belief—and therefore of ecclesial boundaries and limits—and more from the desire to help people nurture each other in the discovery of what it means to be more fully human. This striving for a resurrected humanity within a community of friendship is surely the proper goal of all the disciples of Jesus.

It may also be that our real home and friends are to be found elsewhere.

Time to explore!

Here are some ideas for you to discuss with friends in your local church or community:

- Do you feel that the church is part of the world, or separate from it? How do you understand Christianity's ambiguity about creation?

- What is there to fear about God? Does faith contain fear?

- What are the issues in your community that make people afraid?

Time for some action!

Here are some suggestions for you to try out:

- What activities can you find in your neighborhood or town that work to "arouse the Human Being" or "resurrect the person"?

- How would you go about creating opportunities in your community for strangers to become friends?

For church leaders:

- To what extent has your ministry enabled you to become more fully alive?

- How does your ministry enable your congregation to nurture each other?

Part 2: A Community That Gives Birth to the Divine in Its Midst

It is not difficult to claim that today's embattled and shrunken church uses too much precious energy arguing over the details of belief rather than becoming a prophetic community that seeks unambiguously to include everyone among its friends and, in turn, to accept the friendship of strangers. Often we Christians have great difficulty with those who are not—like us—"in Christ" (Gal 3:25-29). And, despite the rhetoric of welcome and inclusivity, churches of all flavors frequently struggle to overcome what Swinton calls the "principle of likeness" (*Resurrecting the Person*, 2000, 147), whereby we marginalize those who are "other" than us in terms of belief, values, background, or lifestyle.

In its defense, of course, the church may tell the gospel stories of how Jesus had table fellowship with Pharisees and "ate with sinners," but the tone and emphasis given these stories are not always ones that highlight any obvious mutuality between those present at such meals. We readily believe that such occasions were all "one-way" affairs, involving people *whom* Jesus addressed and *to whom* he ministered. We enthusiastically imagine these people eagerly listening to Jesus, mending their ways, and then "turning to the Lord." And consequently we are encouraged to use these stories as models for our own mission and outreach: go out, preach the word, and bring people to Christ. A one-way transaction with little if any suggestion that we might have things to learn or, indeed, that we might need to change our view of things in the light of our encounters with others.

Being the Guests of Others

When Jesus famously sends his disciples out into the world to preach the kingdom of God he tells them to stay in people's homes. In Matthew's story of Jesus sending the "twelve apostles" (10:1-15), we read:

> "Whatever town or village you enter, find out who in it is worthy, and stay there until you leave. As you enter the house, greet it. If the house is worthy, let your peace come upon it; but if it is not worthy, let your peace return to you. If anyone will not welcome you or listen to your words, shake off the dust from your feet as you leave that house or town. Truly I tell you, it will be more tolerable for the land of Sodom and Gomorrah on the day of judgment than for that town" (11-15).

And in Luke's account of the "mission of the seventy" (10:1-20) Jesus says:

> "Whatever house you enter, first say, 'Peace to this house!' And if anyone is there who shares in peace, your peace will rest on that person; but if not, it will return to you. Remain in the same house, eating and drinking whatever they provide, for the laborer deserves to be paid. Do not move about from house to house. Whenever you enter a town and its people welcome you, eat what is set before you; cure the sick who are there, and say to them, 'The kingdom of God has come near to you.' But whenever you enter a town and they do not welcome you, go out into its streets and say, 'Even the dust of your town that clings to our feet, we wipe off in protest against you. Yet know this: the kingdom of God has come near.' I tell you, on that day it will be more tolerable for Sodom than for that town" (5-12).

While the church has emphasized the disciples being sent out to "proclaim the gospel to non-believers," an equally urgent reading today is one that stresses the need to go and *become the guests of other people* in their homes, neighborhoods, and communities.

Matthew has Jesus say "whatever town or village you enter, find out who in it is worthy" (10:11), and, "If the house is worthy, let your peace come upon it …" (13). Luke reverses the order: "whatever house you enter, first say, 'Peace to this house!' And if anyone is there who shares in peace, your peace will rest on that person" (5-6a). Both gospels link "worthiness" with the presence of "peace"—"shalom, wholeness, completeness"—in a way that suggests that "worthy," ("axios"), has less to do with a moral judgment of the inhabitants' "worthiness" and more to do with congruity. In other words, Jesus tells his disciples to discover those places where "peace" is already to be found, and then to stay there, dwelling among those people and living out the "shalom" that both the disciples *and their hosts* have to share in common.

That this task of *mutual revelatory hospitality* is urgent is, for both Matthew and Luke, encapsulated in Jesus saying that "it will be more tolerable for Sodom [and Gomorrah] than for that town" (Mt 10:15; Lk 10:12). A reference not only to the infamous violation of the hospitality code in those places, but also—by the usage of Jesus' day—a reminder of the swift "inevitability of divine vengeance" *for those who ignore it.* (See Knust, *Unprotected Texts,* 2011, 167.)

For in becoming the guests of others, both guest and host discover *together* what it means to live in divine hospitality and so create a *habit* of "mutuality, co-operation, and companionship" (De La Torre, *A Lily Among Thorns,* 2007, 183) or what Brueggemann calls "a new humanness, rooted in holiness and practiced in neighborliness" (Brueggemann, *The Word Militant,* 2007b, 34).

Spiritual Dialogue

The challenge of being the guests of others, to be invited into their "sacred space"—whether in their home, work space, or place of worship—is one that requires us to relearn how to experience other people as subjects, and not as objects. In terms of traditional Christian mission, this means to encounter other people not merely as the *object* of our efforts to convert them, but rather as the *potential source of divine revelation* in their own persons. They are people in whom God is to be encountered.

At the heart of this challenge to discover the divine in the nurture of neighborliness, mutuality, and a common life is, of course, the task of conversation and dialogue. For too long we have satisfied ourselves chiefly with apologetic monologues, and are then surprised to discover that people have ceased listening to us! The time has come to rediscover the true nature and value of "correlational dialogue" (O'Leary, *Lost Soul?* 1999, 201) and the possibilities it holds for a risk-shaped ministry: a model of ministry that encourages conversations that open all parties to the possibility of transformation; what Morisy calls "connecting across boundaries" (Morisy, *Bothered and Bewildered*, 2009, 37).

These boundaries will include that of language itself. If, as Firet reminds us, God speaks "in our mother tongue" (Firet, *Dynamics in Pastoring*, 1986, 97)—if our first experiences of God are inevitably in the language of our own family, community, and culture—it is clear that we will need to become, at least to some extent, bilingual if we want to properly understand the experience of others, although, as any linguist knows, the key to understanding other languages is not so much the knack of translating from one language to another, but rather the ability to *think in the other language*. This, in turn, requires the mental effort to adopt and use the other's frame of reference.

Becoming fluently bi- or even multi-lingual in this way, that we might learn to listen across difference and rediscover the lost art of "conversation across boundaries," is not to limit ourselves to listening and speaking. It suggests also the human vocation to action, participation, and mutual involvement in the lives and experience of other people that is mirrored in the heart of the (Christian) understanding of God, where Father, Son, and Holy Spirit participate in a mutual exchange or "dance" of creative energy and transformative activity. (See Fiddes, *Participating in God* in Ward, *Participation and Mediation*, 2008, 27.)

While in many places, of course, Christians are already at the forefront of such creative interactions, all too often such "outreach activities" are still a one-directional process aimed solely at drawing people in, rather than at discovering and naming the divine already at work in the world, learning from how others experience and celebrate it, and then taking that wisdom back into the church for its ongoing transformation. That this is far from common practice is a tragic failure of imagination in the institution of the church. It is the result of a dominant theology that is generally unaccustomed to recognizing the face of God and the mark of authentic divine action in what lies outside the constraints of its doctrinal worldview in difference, otherness, and strangeness.

At Home with Difference

Creation reveals that all difference, otherness, and "strangeness" originate in God, and that divinity is, therefore, *inherently bound up with difference in all its forms.* Despite this, all too often we persist in shying nervously away from what is different, strange, and "unlike us." Often this includes an inability to recognize the strangeness of God's presence and action in the world, which then further confines us to operating within the bounds of sameness and familiarity.

A dominant and persistent theme of both the Torah and the Christian gospels is, however, that the stranger is to be welcomed at all costs. For the Bible is insistent that the stranger, the alien (literally the "other"), is always a concrete embodiment of the mysterious divine presence among us, as we read in the Torah:

> When an alien resides with you in your land, you shall not oppress the alien. The alien who resides with you shall be to you as the citizen among you; you shall love the alien as yourself, for you were aliens in the land of Egypt: I am the Lord your God (Lev 19:33-34).

Later in Hebrews we read: "Do not neglect to show hospitality to strangers, for by doing that some have entertained angels without knowing it" (13:2).

To fully appreciate the presence of God and to respond creatively to the divine in our midst requires us to create an effective mechanism for engaging with the stranger, one which opens us up to the risk of embracing "whom" and "what" may be completely unknown and therefore also potentially dangerous. At the same time, it may allow us to discover and explore a deep mutuality as we share what we are with each other.

A way of doing this that is familiar to us from the story of Abraham and Sarah, and elsewhere in Scripture, is the tradition of radical hospitality:

> The Lord appeared to Abraham by the oaks of Mamre, as he sat at the entrance of his tent in the heat of the day. He looked up and saw three men standing near him. When he saw them, he ran from the tent entrance to meet them, and bowed down to the ground. He said, "My lord, if I find favor with

you, do not pass by your servant. Let a little water be brought, and wash your feet, and rest yourselves under the tree. Let me bring a little bread, that you may refresh yourselves, and after that you may pass on— since you have come to your servant." So they said, "Do as you have said." And Abraham hastened into the tent to Sarah, and said, "Make ready quickly three measures of choice flour, knead it, and make cakes." Abraham ran to the herd, and took a calf, tender and good, and gave it to the servant, who hastened to prepare it. Then he took curds and milk and the calf that he had prepared, and set it before them; and he stood by them under the tree while they ate (Gen 18:1-8).

Here the performance of the sacred rituals of hospitality—the host's greeting and bowing to the ground and the guest's acceptance of foot washing and refreshment— creates a space that diffuses the shock of difference and minimizes the potential danger by the sharing of mutual vulnerability. Thus the risk is run by all parties and the shared benefits made manifest. In this story the risky space of encounter is under a tree at the entrance to Abraham's tent. It is a space that is not inside the privacy of the home, nor outside the safety of the immediate encampment, but rather in an intermediate and liminal space.

A Generative Space

Such spaces offer the possibility of encounter where strangers can meet together without undue threat and where their different identities may overlap without blurring or diminishing their distinctness.

Such in-between spaces have been likened to the stairwells in shared residential buildings that are not the private secure spaces where people live, but rather spaces that all may pass through: spaces that are open to multiple identities and encounters with strangers. (See Bhabha, *The Location of Culture*, 1994, 5.) Here the stairwell represents a kind of "commons" that, while never devoid of potential risk, is by definition available to all groups and may give rise to all sorts of creative interactions. Indian Dalit theologian Jacob Devadason is developing the idea of "verandah theology." As with the stairwell, the verandah is understood to be neither inside nor outside the home. It is a space where neighbors and strangers alike may be encountered and welcomed in the safe environment assured by the rules of hospitality, and where difference may be explored without threat.

These encounters—whether between people of different faiths or between those of faith and other "spiritual seekers"—create the possibility of creative conversations that allow people to explore and share their experience of being alive in the world, as well as their search for meaning and purpose, and so enable divinity to be named in all its startling and simple diversity.

Difference and the Possibility of Change

While the urgency of this task for today's fractured world cannot be underestimated, it needs also to be acknowledged that such interactions are, for some people, enormously threatening. They may challenge deeply cherished beliefs and values, and so threaten, only to force people to further retreat into defensive and belligerent attitudes.

Even so, the potential destabilization of these encounters is held in tension, for both host and guest, by its location in the dynamic "in-betweeness" that is neutral ground, neither inside nor outside, a safe space that is open to newness and difference. Consequently, the possibility for creative conversation about God, and the mutual naming of particular understandings of the divine, enable an exploration of difference which, by virtue of its location, is not about coercion, conversion, or competitive maneuvering, but about creating instead a "ferment" (Randriamampionona, *Difference as Ferment for the Hybrid Church, passim*) that opens up the possibility of movement and change.

Listening to, and sharing, new perspectives and fresh insights into other people's experience encourages transformative relationships and the creation of communities of wise practice that the world needs right now. Time and again, the scriptural witness itself is that God always intervenes creatively in such in-between spaces, moments, and encounters. As friends and strangers, insiders and outsiders alike, risk experiencing such moments of potential destabilization, chaos, and collapse, we discover that God is present in our midst, transforming hitherto suspect and negative understandings, motivations, and interactions into opportunities for new beginnings, (not least in the story of the crucifixion and resurrection!). As we seek to co-operate with divine activity in the world in this way, we discover ourselves transformed into instruments of blessing for the future of the whole human family.

Can the Church Be Such a Place of Encounter?

As long as the church is content to keep its gaze largely on its internal disagreements and doctrinal differences, on issues of self-image and status, it will be unchallenged and unaffected by the need to engage with its God-given vocation to be a place of encounter and discovery and to develop a dynamic ministry of human transformation such as envisioned here, a ministry that seeks to learn as much from others as it wishes to share with them, and so—together with others—become an instrument of healing for the world. For the task of creating radical transformative friendship, and the use of prophetic and imaginative engagement across differences as a means to local and global change, is needed today as never before.

Such a ministry would also prove to be a source of rediscovery and deep renewal for Christian communities everywhere. Authentic encounter with otherness inevitably serves to deepen our understanding of, and commitment to, our own faith and religious practice. To undertake such a ministry is to rededicate ourselves to discovering, embodying, and sharing all that we might imagine Jesus to mean when he speaks of "fullness of life" or of having "life and hav[ing] it abundantly" (Jn 10:10).

For what does "fullness of life" mean if not the discovery, creation, and sharing of the possibilities for a greater personhood for all humanity? This "fullness of life" provides a greater understanding of what it means to be human with the robust potential to engage with the needs of today's global human family, our fractured communities of difference, and the challenges of equitably sharing space and resources in an increasingly fragile world.

Towards a Greater Personhood

The imperative for transformative global friendship is a particular summons for Christian communities everywhere to step out on the journey towards embracing the vision of greater personhood that awaits us all. For Jesus, as witnessed in his own healing ministry, calls us time and again to engage with the potential for a restored, renewed, and enlivened humanity and to "arouse the Human Being" (Wink, 2002) in us all; to let "Him-Her" inspire new patterns of human living, new challenges for the human community, and tangible new hope for the world.

For to live faithfully as religious people, as the world's faith communities seek to do, is to be determined to identify with, participate in, and transform the struggles and suffering of people everywhere, and—together with all people of good will—to work to raise the benchmark so all can participate in a life of abundance and flourishing; to create "another possible world" (Althaus-Reid, *From Feminist Theology to Indecent Theology, passim*) here on earth in our own time, before we dare dream of just rewards elsewhere or in an afterlife. To dare to dream of greater personhood for all people, to aspire to discover ourselves to be truly sons and daughters of the "One Creator God"—as "sacred selves" who can experience re-enchantment, delight, and reconnection to our divine origins—is to become a community of irresistible radical friendship that is indeed capable of giving birth to the divine in its midst.

As we journey together to that end and deeper into the transformative mystery of God, we are inevitably invited to honor God's presence among us in the only possible way: with worship and celebration, that all people everywhere might together say "Amen!"

Time to explore!

Here are some ideas for you to discuss with friends in your local church or community:

- With some people from your church, visit the place of worship of another religion. Experience what it is to be a guest there. If you can, sit at the back as they worship. Be respectful, but alert to what you feel. Share together afterwards.

- Ask a group from a different religion to visit your church. Offer hospitality; encourage questions; invite them to experience your worship. Share together afterwards. What did you experience?

- What do the terms "greater personhood" and "Human Being" mean to you?

Time for some action!

Here are some suggestions for you to try out:

- Where are the "stairwell" or "verandah" spaces in your own community: the common ground shared by all? What activities might you organize to bring together radically different groups? What would you seek to achieve to benefit your community?

- How might such activities explore the notion of "greater personhood" and "Human Being"?

For church leaders:

- How is your church a space for safe and creative encounter between different groups?

- Where have you encountered human flourishing in your community? How does your ministry enable other people to experience "life in all its fullness"?

- How do you experience fullness of life?

CHAPTER 5

"Celebrate!"

Part 1: Celebration

"Life is for living," someone once said. And indeed it is. The sad truth of the matter, however, is that for the majority of people in our world today, life is a tremendous struggle. For any who dare to call ourselves religious—no matter what our religion might be—our shared task is surely to make every urgent effort we can to alleviate the grinding, energy-sapping poverty of our brothers and sisters across the globe, and to do our utmost to enable them to flourish, as we expect to. There can be no excuse.

Poverty and social disadvantage do not, of course, exclude the possibility of moments of celebration and opportunities for thanksgiving, as anyone who has lived in that world will have discovered. Indeed, "westerners" can learn much about the art of celebration and thanksgiving from people living on or below the breadline, *wherever* they are in the world. Unfortunately, many of us have lost sense of the meaning behind the idea of both celebration and thanksgiving.

Thanksgiving has become somewhat problematic for many people. Saying "thank you"—expressing gratitude—to others, or to God, often seems somehow strangely at odds with our contemporary consumerist culture, since it emphasizes our dependency; and while it is true that we do ultimately rely on other people for all sorts of things, it can be a deeply discomforting thought for those of us who might prefer to imagine ourselves to be totally self-reliant. "Why should we say thank you? What we have, we have worked for, or got by our own efforts, or deserve, or have *by rights*."

Thanksgiving may, of course, still have a role to play as an *expression of relief* when some potential catastrophe fails, after all, to materialize. We might say: "I was really thankful that … " or "I was grateful for …." But thankfulness and gratitude in these cases sound like little more than abstract turns of phrase. Who exactly is being thanked here?

Jesus Gives Thanks

In the stories of the "feeding the four thousand" Jesus famously gives thanks to God:

> In those days when there was again a great crowd without anything to eat, he called his disciples and said to them, "I have compassion for the crowd, because they have been with me now for three days and have nothing to eat. If I send them away hungry to their homes, they will faint on the way—and some of them have come from a great distance." His disciples replied, "How can one feed these people with bread here in the desert?" He asked them, "How many loaves do you have?" They said, "Seven." Then he ordered the crowd to sit down on the ground; and he took the seven loaves, *and after giving thanks he broke them and gave them to his disciples to distribute*; and they distributed them to the crowd. They had also a few small fish; and after blessing them, he ordered that these too should be distributed. They ate and were filled; and they took up the broken pieces left over, seven baskets full. Now there were about four thousand people. And he sent them away (Mk 8:1-19, my emphasis; see also Mt 15:32-39).

This narrative is an interesting one. It presents the disciples with a dilemma: a great crowd without anything to eat. Jesus highlights the urgency of the situation: "if I send them away hungry to their homes, they will faint on the way

…." This then sends the disciples into a panic: "How can one feed these people …?" It is a question of too many people and simply too few resources. At this point, Jesus takes what there is—seven loaves—and gives thanks. He then passes the bread to his disciples to distribute. And there is enough for all.

However else we might understand this story, what's strongly suggested is that the act of thanksgiving for what there is already becomes the moment of transformation into "something more," into plenty, into abundance, into gratuitous overflowing: "They ate and were filled; and they took up the broken pieces left over, seven baskets full." Jesus gives thanks for what there already is, and then more is provided.

The grateful recognition of something to share—be it by divine miracle or by the simple effect of embarrassing others to donate what they were keeping to themselves—provokes a reaction that serves to underscore the necessary communal dimension of society, and of human responses to the demands and injustices of daily life. For, whether or not we believe that there is someone to thank, the act of thanksgiving for what has been given—for what we already have, no matter how little—can become the touchstone for lessening our sense of dissatisfaction with what we do not have. It creates a deeper sense of appreciation of what we have already received. Such thanksgiving helps mitigate our seemingly eternal hunger, longings, desires, and frustrations about what we do not and cannot have. It opens the door to celebration.

So to Celebration

If our understanding of the nature of thanksgiving has become dulled and distorted, then something similar can surely be said of our practices around celebration. All too often in our contemporary understanding celebration has become deeply associated with consumption. We feel we cannot celebrate without consuming inordinate quantities of food, drink, or "things." Nor can we celebrate without spending large amounts of money and resources, because the quality of the celebration is all too frequently gauged in direct proportion to the level of consumption. We, in turn, often feel obliged to express our feelings, affection, and even love, by the ever greater quantity and relative cost of the gifts and offerings we bring.

This observation is not in any way made to demean or condemn celebration. We *need* to be able to celebrate. But, as Dorothee Soelle has noted, the church's historic fear of enjoyment and its reluctance to celebrate has not won it any friends, despite all that there is in the world to celebrate! Soelle calls it "a kind of spiritual suicide" (*The Silent Cry*, 2001, 18).

Thanksgiving and celebration occur both when ordinary random moments become transfigured by a sense of their extraordinariness, and when the cyclical rhythms of life are seen against the linear time trajectory that orders our daily life and world. Thanksgiving and celebration occur at points of intersection: between the individual and the group or community, the past and the present, the ordinary and extraordinary, the here and now and what is not here and now, the immanent and the transcendent. They are moments of pause amid the flow of life, when ordinary time— "*chronos*"—becomes "*kairos*": those moments of grace and gift when time seems to stand still and extraordinary things happen.

Thanksgiving and celebration are about the individual's connection or relationship with others, the world, and the universe, and with the impact these things have on the individual and the community. They are opportunities for connecting with—remembering, recalling, and commemorating—the past and anticipating or imagining the future. They situate a person, group, or community within a particular time frame while also lifting them outside time to a place within the bigger picture of eternity. While they look to commemorate what is special, thanksgiving and celebration also ultimately serve to emphasize the point that life is about "being alive in every moment and not just a few of them" (Soelle, 177).

Reclaiming Thanksgiving and Celebration

One of the key elements in any risk-shaped ministry must surely be a willingness to encourage people to explore their own experience, give thanks for what has already been, and make the connections between their everyday living and the deep human need to celebrate; for life has become, for so many people in our communities, utterly trivialized. Life has become one endless round of production and consumption (or else marginalization and exclusion) without any respite or time to simply stand still and give thanks. Life has become dulled daily by consumerism, anxiety, and a deep loss of connection to those things that give life meaning.

What undergirds thanksgiving and celebration is the embodied nature of human experience and desire. A key task, therefore, for Christians wishing to serve their community *and* church will be—as we saw in Chapter One—to learn how to celebrate human experience and sketch out a deep understanding of the place of desire in our lives and communities. For experience is the benchmark of existence, and desire is the motivational force for most of the things we do. And though both experience and desire can become distorted and pathological, they are ultimately "God-given" and an intimate part of who we are called to be as "Human Beings."

This is important, as we shall see. Unless we learn how to properly give thanks and celebrate, then we cannot really understand what it means to worship.

Catching a Different Vision

One of the key modern contributions to our understanding of the meaning of Jesus is that of René Girard. He views the crucified Jesus as bringing a permanent end to the cycle of needing to blame, scapegoat, and punish that has so characterized human behavior.

This vicious circle of retaliation is perpetuated by the tendency we all have to copy each other. Girard calls it "mimetic violence." Because we are motivated by fear and envy and cannot get everything our own way, or acquire or achieve everything we lack or desire, we resort to violent and selfish behaviors in our attempts to fulfill our ambitions. Others then copy and re-enact these: parent to child, community to community, nation to nation. Perhaps mimetic violence is the ultimate sin that is visited "to the third and fourth generation" (Deut 5:9) of humanity!

This does then beg the question of whether the opposite—*virtuous* circles—might themselves be created, experienced, and then also imitated and shared. In particular, Girard asks whether the "Sermon on the Mount" might itself, for instance, be one text that sees Jesus seeking to combat mimetic violence by identifying and naming its root causes. (See Kirwan, *Discovering Gerard*, 2004, 77.) Girard sees Jesus as encouraging his listeners to "break the cycle of retributive violence" (Kirwan, 2004, 77) by finding the resolution of their anger and pain, not in aggression, violence, material things, or frustrated status, but rather in experiencing blessedness:

"Blessed are the poor in spirit, for theirs is the kingdom of heaven.

"Blessed are those who mourn, for they will be comforted.

"Blessed are the meek, for they will inherit the earth.

"Blessed are those who hunger and thirst for righteousness, for they will be filled.

"Blessed are the merciful, for they will receive mercy.

"Blessed are the pure in heart, for they will see God.

"Blessed are the peacemakers, for they will be called children of God.

"Blessed are those who are persecuted for righteousness' sake, for theirs is the kingdom of heaven.

"Blessed are you when people revile you and persecute you and utter all kinds of evil against you falsely on my account" (Mt 5:3-11).

The reasons for our resentment are only implied in the text: death, disinheritance, injustice, covetousness, warfare, persecution. But, following Girard's reading, it becomes possible to see that Jesus' encouragement to find resolution of these experiences by seeking blessedness and happiness—and not retribution—may, in turn, become a new and re-creative pattern for human relationships and interactions; a circle of virtuous action that is *not* founded on fear or envy, but on the embodied and shared experience of blessedness. Lives that are resourced by the experience of God's boundless and bountiful blessing—and in communicating that experience with others—are lives that are open to thanksgiving, celebration, and, indeed, worship.

Something of the impact of this different vision, this virtuous circle, may be seen in the description by Luke of a community empowered by the post-resurrection experience of blessedness:

Awe came upon everyone, because many wonders and signs were being done by the apostles. All who believed were together and had all things in common; they would sell their possessions and goods and distribute the proceeds to all, as any had need. Day by day, as they spent much time together in the temple, they broke bread at home and ate their food with glad and generous hearts, praising God and having the goodwill of all the people. And day by day the Lord added to their number those who were being saved (Acts 2:43-47).

Sharing Experiences of Blessedness

If the Christian experience of God's blessing is authentic, then it follows that Christian communities will find themselves acting out this generosity among themselves, and—more especially and urgently—among others, not only in the ways they have experienced blessing, but in their willingness to recognize, name, and celebrate the presence of God's love and blessing elsewhere, *in whatever form it is manifested.* Divine blessing can never be limited to, or solely defined by, the Christian community. One very creative task for the church lies, therefore, in recognizing and naming these other expressions of love and blessedness, wherever and however they are to be found.

Two small but pertinent examples are described in the work of Daniel White Hodge (*No Church in the Wild*, 2013) in the US and Chris Shannahan (*NEET Believers?*, 2012) in the UK. Focusing on Hip Hop culture as a vehicle for belief and religious expression among the young urban unemployed, both authors explore the changed nature of "belief" and how this is articulated outside the Christian community and church structures. In these marginalized social groups, the experience of meaning, connection, and hope is celebrated through contemporary musical culture. This serves both as an expression of their experience of disenchantment and frustrated desire, and also of their perception of Jesus ("Jesuz") as an inspirational icon and source of empowerment. This empowerment—"blessedness" in religious terms— is experienced as group solidarity, attachment to their neighborhood, and "sacred actions" (Shannahan, 327) such as sharing the rap music they have created. As Shannahan indicates, the experience of those marginalized by mainstream society and religious communities "might open new windows onto the nature of liberative spiritualities" (319), that can challenge existing norms about the "performance of belief" (See Shannahan, 331). These groups have a great deal to teach us!

Virtuous Circles of Blessing

While such celebrations of "belief" and spiritual experience in the face of exclusion might resonate with Jesus' message to the marginalized of his own day, sadly they may seem alien to contemporary church-goers. Indeed, they may not appear as being in any way consonant with established ideas about belief and spiritual experience; but that's surely the whole point.

For while the church may be happy to function within established or revealed parameters for the performance of its faith, the task for any risk-shaped ministry is to seek out and join in the celebration of human experience wherever it is found. This will involve listening attentively to the ways in which desire (fulfilled or frustrated) is articulated, and then— while exploring this as a different, though not necessarily inauthentic, experience of blessedness—seek to engage with it as part of the process of the building up of the kingdom-kindom of God, co-operating with God to create virtuous circles of blessing that are poured out into the world.

Crucially, it is only by the Christian community, acting out God's generous blessing, intentionally and in such creative and prophetic ways—and in being open to *receiving* blessing from the most unexpected of places—that the church will be able to avoid withering away and ceasing to bear fruit.

Fruitfulness

For fruitfulness "occurs, where God is enjoyed" (Soelle, 302). It does not matter how "God" is defined, and whether or not this enjoyment happens in urban environments, on the margins of our communities, or within the hallowed precincts of our places of worship.

However, enjoyment—and, more fundamentally, fruitfulness—are not experiences routinely associated with church life or Christian community, nor particularly are related ideas such as "awe," "delight," "playfulness," and "creativity." Yet all of these are component parts of thanksgiving and celebration. All are characteristic of the fruitfulness that flows from the experience of God's presence among us.

If the church is to continue to anticipate outsiders attending for worship, then it needs to prepare the ground by exploring how enjoyment, awe, delight, playfulness, and creativity—all characteristics of fruitfulness—are experienced (or not!) in what it offers. While few people will expect liturgy, ritual, and worship to be entertainment in the ordinary sense; awe, enjoyment, delight, playfulness, and creativity are the essential ingredients that make for rich and transformative experiences of thanksgiving and celebration.

How, then, might these ingredients translate into ways of informing, enriching, and promoting the experience of worship of the divine?

Time to explore!

Here are some ideas for you to discuss with friends in your local church or community:

- When did you last give thanks? What was the reason?

- What does celebration mean for you?

- How do you understand the Sermon on the Mount?

- How can people "enjoy" God?

Time for some action!

Here are some suggestions for you to try out:

- What experience of God's blessing or empowerment can your church share with others?

- Go out into your community and find those places and times where people are celebrating life in ways that are different from what happens in church. What can your church learn from this?

- How might the church incorporate some of the richness of these experiences?

For church leaders:

- How might your church work with the local community to create virtuous circles of blessing in your neighborhood?

- How, in your experience, does the church enable people to "enjoy God"?

- How does your ministry assist people in experiencing or creating fruitfulness?

Part 2: Worship

What Is It All About?

Many years ago, a Christian friend told me that he "needed to worship." At the time, I found his exact meaning—and the whole business of worship—quite beyond me. To some extent I still do, but perhaps this statement needs some unpacking.

It is traditionally understood in most parts of the church that prayer and worship should have four basic ingredients: adoration, confession, thanksgiving, and supplication. The purpose of these things is primarily to "give glory" to God. So, in each act of Christian worship, as we celebrate God's presence among us in word and sacrament, we celebrate God's majesty, greatness, and splendor. We adore God. We give thanks for all that God does. We confess our own sinfulness. We ask for God's forgiveness, intercession, healing, and blessing for ourselves and for other people and situations in the world. In doing these things we *glorify* God.

Glory is understood to be the manifestation of the presence and action of God in the world: God's "reputation" or "fame" (Greek "*doxa*"). It is often associated with intense light, brightness, brilliance, resplendence. In response to this manifestation of glory, we in turn glorify God—we offer glory to God—in our worship. Indeed, we can also say that we share in God's glory when we let the image of God in us shine out in the world through our own actions. We can reflect God's glory, albeit in a necessarily limited manner.

Moreover, the whole shape and content of the liturgy— the readings from Scripture and the sermon or homily—are designed to reinforce the underlying traditional theological worldview that sees fallen humanity reliant upon redemption by Jesus in order to be restored and made at one again with God. This is the reason why God deserves to receive glory.

But this customary view is being increasingly questioned by some people: indeed, by practicing Christians of all denominations. While it may be said that worship is a *free act* of thanksgiving to God that seeks to glorify God and celebrate human liberation, the way in which "authorized" liturgies are used to reinforce "orthodox" theology—and vice versa—seems only to result in the creation of another vicious circle, one that actually works against human liberation.

This claim rests on two premises. The first is that the repetition and remembrance of the process of redemption that is at the heart of eucharistic theology effectively creates an endlessly reinforced expectation of needing to confess sin and start over and over again. The second is that, though God already has all the glory, the desire to give God more glory is bound up with our perception of the need to placate God's wrath and keep God "sweet," despite the fact that redemption has taken place.

In this uncomfortable view, worship is nothing more than a *vicious* circle because—while it may, perhaps, allow us to feel we are "temporarily better people," it generally fails to change our world view. It merely reinforces the status quo— the fallenness of humanity and creation—and fails to allow people to see themselves and the world through another lens, through the eyes and mind of God; and so come to experience liberation—resurrection living—and discover the essential blessedness of all of creation, people included.

While this may be grossly oversimplifying the case, it does seem to be what many ordinary church-goers understand is going on. At least, it is how they understand what they imagine they are supposed to understand about worship. It does, arguably, also sound a chord with the rather cynical judgment that "all our church ever expects from us is attendance and tithing …" (Frost and Hirsch, *The Faith of Leap*, 2011, 99).

Might it be possible to understand, instead, how worship can become a virtuous circle?

Through a New Lens

Worship (originally "worth-ship") is surely better seen as a time in which we allow this new lens—the "God perspective"—to challenge our own view of ourselves and the world. It is an opportunity for the "God-stories" to become the frame of reference for recognizing the *true worth* of things, not the stories that the world—or the church— tells us. It is a chance for the real truth of things to become revealed, visible, and no longer hidden. Worship is then a space in which we allow ourselves to fall under the spell of the Gospel—for us to become "God-spelled"—and so able to experience and trust God as Jesus did. It is an occasion for being gripped, transfixed, and transfigured by those gestalts and "aha! moments" we have spoken of earlier.

In this view worship is a *virtuous* circle, for it allows us to see ourselves and creation differently. Worship becomes the reason for, and the expression of, a deep gratitude that, thanks to "God" (or the "God perspective" or "fresh frame of reference," call it what we will), we are able to experience a new and transformative way of being, one that liberates us by changing how we understand ourselves, how we see the universe, and how we relate to—and care for—all humanity and creation. Worship is about the discovery of our true selves and the true nature of things: a revelation that then cascades out into the universe.

Opening up the Box

Just as we observed earlier that life has become trivialized, so now we can add that, all too frequently, institutional worship has been dumbed-down and tamed into being a "polite hermeneutic" (Brueggemann, *The Message of the*

Psalms, 1984, 16). We may now also begin to understand how Dorothee Soelle (referencing in part the German mystic Thomas Müntzer) can claim that the church prefers a "fictitious" faith—*composed of facts and stories*—since a "fictitious faith ... is fine for the head and keeps the institution functioning" (2001, 2). When mediated through the church, such a faith tends to limit human experience of the divine to one that fits only the institutional box and its theological self-understanding. Indeed, Soelle goes even further, by suggesting that, "the experience of divine presence no longer happens through the mediation of doctrine, sacred text, or sacrament" (15); and that the divine is now *only* to be encountered and experienced outside the church and its institutional forms of belief and worship.

Perhaps only worship that is *untamed* (or "indecent," to reference Althaus-Reid, 2004) and willing to step outside the safe "decency" of the "polite hermeneutical box" and create a virtuous circle of experience is able to connect people into a bigger frame of reference and meaning. There it is possible to experience worship that is no longer bound to the merely "fictitious," but is instead envisioned as a *space for generating the spiritual adventure of a life time.*

What would such a space look like?

Into the Wildness of God

In response to Beck's assertion that, in the space created by organized religion, we "chain our personal God to our own desires, traumas, hysterias, fears and hopes ... [and that we need] to escape the temptation of debasing our own God, changing Him into a tame, cuddly God" (Beck, *A God of One's Own*, 2010, 13), Soelle's solution is clear. The future of religion, belief, and worship is to be found in mysticism: in experience of the wildness—the "untamedness"—of God.

"Mysticism" has had a very bad press for a long time. On one level the very language with which mystics express themselves appears to resist—or even deny—orthodox interpretation, practice, and belief. Meister Eckhart's famous "I pray God to rid me of God" (Pfeiffer, *Meister Eckhart*, 1956, 220), to quote one famous but not untypical assertion, seems initially suspect. In reality, it is an expression of the experience of having journeyed beyond what is already known and named about God—as defined by the church—to a place where God discloses the "yet-more" and the "otherness" of God.

It is not surprising, therefore, that mystical experience has been frequently condemned by the church as a *dangerous activity* because it is perceived as removing individuals from institutional control, placing them outside the ordinary moral and ethical demands of "right and wrong" and of doctrinal orthodoxy, and freeing them of any requirement to live in "the real world." The history of Christianity is indeed littered with stories of mystics who have been misunderstood, fallen foul of church authorities, and then been condemned. Soelle's comment, for instance, that "Mysticism and organized religion are related like spirit to power" (46) itself illustrates the continuingly disparaging, if pertinent, critique of the church's ways of being in the world that is typically made by those from its mystical traditions, as well as explaining the church's harsh judgment of them.

"Without a Why or a Wherefore"

Perhaps most problematic of all for the institutional church is the simple but widespread assertion, repeated across the spectrum of its mystical traditions, that "God … is common to all" (John Ruusbroec, *The Spiritual Espousals*, 1985, 102). The mystics assert that *all people* can experience God, no matter who they are. "[E]veryone has a share in the power of life" (Soelle, 128), and, since God neither coerces nor condemns, everyone is free to approach God "without a why or a wherefore" (Soelle, 59-62), without concern for outcomes, or the need to placate God or curry favour. We can rest in God's presence as tranquilly and securely as the "lilies in the field" (Mt 6:28), "without a why or wherefore." For as Soelle comments, "in praising the moon as it rises, in praising someone who is loved or, indeed, in praising the source of all good, *the ego that is possessed by goals and craves dominance vanishes. It has stepped outside of itself*" (61, my emphasis).

When worship happens gratuitously, without any ulterior motive, without reference to institutional control or doctrinal orthodoxy, dominance, or dogma, "without a why or a wherefore," people experience transcendence. We step outside our egos and encounter God.

So what would our worship be like if it were done "without a why or a wherefore"? What might happen if the church were to encourage more of a mystical dimension in its life and worship; if the church and its people were nourished by "the edible bread of mysticism" (Soelle, 49)?

Revaluing Words

While it would not necessarily follow that worship infused with a mystical dimension would become wordless, it is clear that the words used would take on a heightened role and significance. While much institutional worship effectively devalues words by their overuse—in contrast to the typical paucity or absence of silence in the liturgy—the acknowledgement that God is ultimately *beyond* all words, language, and definitions brings a freedom from the need to express experience and belief propositionally, uniformly, and according to tradition or convention.

In this way, worship is freed to become something quite different and new. It is released from the expectation of articulating and conveying merely "fictitious" faith. It is freed from forever expressing our dependence on a contractual relationship between self and God, the vicious circle of which we spoke just now. Worship becomes, instead, a place for being encountered by the God *beyond all material expectations*, and a space for exposure to something much more profound.

Imagine this as an objective for a renewed and risk-shaped ministry!

Radical Amazement

Worship that is freed from such contractual expectations—that is offered "without a why or a wherefore"—is opened up to being a virtuous circle that enables people to explore and experience awe, delight, wonder, and radical amazement at our very existence and createdness. Worship would be specifically intended to lead us outside the safety of the box and so help us explore and experience more of our true selves and the true worth of things. It would reveal corrected perspectives and insights, allowing us to discern the things that really do need confessing, forgiving, and letting go, and also disclosing the many formerly hidden and overlooked aspects of our lives that need to be properly named and celebrated.

Such worship would lift us outside our ego-self and its narrow focus and allow us to reconnect with nature, the planet, and our universe. It would help us recognize and affirm our relationship with all living things and embrace our interdependency with the rest of creation. A church reinvigorated with the resultant experience of awe and delight, and familiarity with wonder and amazement, would become a beacon of hope and celebration within its local community.

Imagine this as an ambition for a renewed and risk-shaped ministry!

Liberated into God's Shalom

Awe and delight, harnessed to wonder and amazement will, in turn, release vast amounts of re-creative energy into the community, as the church comes to fully appreciate, perhaps for the first time in a very long time, the true meaning of the Scripture that calls Jesus the "first born" exemplar of "all the fullness of God" (Col 1:19). As Wink reminds us, not only is "Jesus [the] eruption of *joie de vivre* from the center of a celebratory universe" (Wink, *The Human Being*, 89), but also, all of his disciples are invited to experience the same.

This "celebratory re-creative energy" is, by definition, releasing and healing. Thus it will allow us not only to finally befriend our embodied nature, but also to more completely understand, marvel at, and integrate our God-given desire and erotic energy within the fullness—"shalom"—of our own being. As a result, the Christian community will be better able to understand and speak the language of desire that so powerfully influences our contemporary society.

Imagine this as an aspiration for a renewed and risk-shaped ministry!

In Joy and Playfulness

"Joy is the ground … [of] mysticism" says Soelle (175). But joy is different than how we generally imagine it. For rather than it being something we feel about something outside ourselves—being *happy about* an event or *glad to receive* some news—the experience of joy, the act of rejoicing, is something that happens from *within our own bodies* and always in the present moment. Because of this, if we wish to more readily experience joy, we need to learn how to be attentive to each moment. We need urgently to practice the art of living in the present; in the here and now.

The failure to *en-joy* the present moment—in the church at least—is due largely to the distraction of the continual strident conversation between past and future time. Though Christianity is indeed, on one level, an essentially future-oriented religion—resurrection, second coming, afterlife—we look constantly and over-exclusively to the past for guidance from revelation, historic tradition, and doctrine. In our determination to always privilege intellectual understanding and propositional forms of belief—"fictitious faith"—we overlook and undervalue people's *actual embodied experience* and enjoyment of God's self-revelation in the present moment and in the world around us.

We not only diminish worship by leaving out the creative, healing, and playful dimensions of joy, but deprive ourselves and our communities of the chance to join with others in the exploration of a fundamental channel of connection to the divine. Consequently, we need to urgently address the issue of our spiritual impoverishment and our inability to be amazed by life and to rejoice.

Imagine this as a focus of a renewed and risk-shaped ministry!

A Nourishing Community

This concern with issues of impoverishment and nourishment—of our inner self, of our churches, and of our communities—is at the heart both of our dilemma and of the opportunity before us. For just as there is enough food produced in the world to feed the global human community, if we could but find a way to ensure equitable access, better distribution, and fairer trading conditions, so too is there a radical and breath-taking abundance of spiritual resource, if only we could unblock some of the things that hold us back from realizing and releasing it. With God *there is always more* than we can imagine or have any right to expect.

The rediscovery that this "always something more" is available and offered to us unconditionally challenges our narrow thinking. Losing ourselves in even the briefest experience of it overwhelms our ego-driven ways of being. Thus, we find ourselves cast up on the shores of a new place where spiritual flourishing and community resilience and creativity are evidence of churches prepared to embrace their vocation as travelers into those dangerous, if alluring, boundary places of experience; places where the divine and human embrace each other and proffer astonishing new possibilities for life.

These journeys begin with the experience of thanksgiving and celebration, and lead to the adventure of worship. For worship, time set aside unconditionally with all that is—with the strange but awesome otherness of God, releases us from the things that hold us captive. It opens up an opportunity for birthing newness: new life, new possibilities, and new hope.

Imagine this, and you have begun to sketch out a renewed, risk-shaped, and immensely creative ministry!

Time to explore!

Here are some ideas for you to discuss with friends in your local church or community:

- What is your experience and understanding of worship? Do you feel that you need to worship? Does it liberate you, or not?

- Do you experience God differently in church worship than you do in the world?

- What do you think about the suggestion that worship is a "space for generating the spiritual adventure of a life time"?

Time for some action!

Here are some suggestions for you to try out:

- Alone, or with a group of friends from your church, list those occasions when you have experienced a sense of: being lifted out of yourself, deeply affected by silence, reconnected with creation or the universe, filled with *joie de vivre* at being alive, or overwhelmed by joy or gratitude.

- Then together, try to work out how to share these experiences with your congregation in an informal act of worship created by your group. Assemble the music, images, words, Scripture, silence, activities, and objects you might use and organize them into a satisfying whole.

For church leaders:

- How do you feel church liturgy and worship does—or does not—engage with the spiritual longings of your congregation?

- In some denominations stepping outside the "authorized" forms of worship may not readily be permitted. But how might you imagine an act of worship along the lines suggested above? What could worship look like if it contained none of the expected elements?

- In an imaginary world, what would be your own preferred form of worship?

CHAPTER 6

Risk-Shaped Ministry

Part 1: Giving Birth to Creativity

New Beginnings

At its heart the Christian faith is all about newness and new beginnings. The Jewish Torah opens with the book Genesis—in Hebrew *Bereshith*, "in the beginning." It describes the creation of humanity, the great "begettings" and genealogies of the patriarchs, and Abraham's journey to find the Promised Land and establish the Hebrew nation. In contrast, the origins of the Christian gospels lie with a spontaneous and unprecedented foundational event of a not dissimilar kind that erupts into time and space and begets a radical new community of equals. We now call this event "the resurrection," and the earliest surviving account of it is the so-called "first ending" of Mark's Gospel:

> When the sabbath was over, Mary Magdalene, and Mary the mother of James, and Salome bought spices, so that they might go and anoint him. And very early on the first day of the week, when the sun had risen, they went to the tomb. They had been saying to one another, "Who will roll away the stone for us from the entrance to the tomb?" When they looked up, they saw that the stone, which was very large, had already been rolled back. As they entered the tomb, they saw a young man, dressed in a white robe, sitting on the right side; and they were alarmed. But he said to them, "Do not be alarmed; you are looking for Jesus of Nazareth, who was crucified. He has been raised; he is not here. Look, there is the place they laid him. But

go, tell his disciples and Peter that he is going ahead of you to Galilee; there you will see him, just as he told you." So they went out and fled from the tomb, for terror and amazement had seized them; and they said nothing to anyone, for they were afraid (Mk 16:1-8).

Now as beginnings go, it's not great. And as a story intended to excite people with the possibilities of a new way of being, it's even worse. But what it does do—and very effectively—is to testify to what happens, and how people react, when novelty and radical newness burst into being. It can be terrifying!

In many ways this account of the women at the tomb is highly reminiscent of the story of the angels and the shepherds from the birth narratives: "… they were terrified. But the angel said to them, 'Do not be afraid; for see—I am bringing you good news of great joy …'" (Lk 2:9-10). This similarity is not surprising, for the birth narratives were not written down until many years after the resurrection event, which itself then formed the lens through which the whole Jesus story was subsequently told.

The sheer novelty of what those women experienced in the garden that morning was—and remains—both "awe-full" and deeply disturbing. It reduced them—and can reduce anyone—to muteness, to a temporary inability to find the words capable of expressing what actually happened. It shocked them to the core. So the women fled the tomb. Terrified, they ran as fast as they could away from the experience. People still do.

Being Alive and Vital

In the previous chapter we talked about the adventure of mystical living that nourishes and re-energizes individuals and communities. We explored the importance of revaluing words, and the impact of radical amazement, and what it would mean to be liberated into God's "shalom" or wholeness. We thought about what the experience of *disconnection* from normality—through some sudden gestalt or joyful revelation—and *reconnection* to the healing reality of the present moment would feel like, as the strange, but overwhelming, "otherness" of God releases us from all that holds us captive and opens us up to a scary encounter with newness. Each of these five elements—revaluing words, radical amazement, liberation into "shalom," the shock of the new, and reconnection to the "awe-full" potential of the present moment—is visible in Mark's earliest account of the "Easter experience."

Unfortunately though, far too many of us focus too much—and sometimes exclusively—on one half of this experience: the "saving death of Jesus." In doing so, we limit our perception of Jesus to be predominantly about "what he did for us on the cross." We effectively make this dark dimension of his story the sole interpretive key and, consequently, we downplay or marginalize the significance and impact of the resurrection itself. All too often we forget that crucifixion and resurrection are two equal and indivisible halves of the same extraordinary event, and when we do this two things happen.

The first is that, instead of celebrating a single liberative event, we allow ourselves to be tied into endlessly replaying Jesus' crucifixion, continually rehearsing our indebtedness and need for redemption, and repeatedly lamenting our "sinful" nature. We effectively create a vicious circle, as we have seen: one that can encourage an almost obsessive dependency on the need for us to ever be redeemed sinners, and nothing more. We get bogged down in the crucifixion and so struggle to realize the significance of the whole event; that the work of redemption is over and done, complete, and fulfilled, "*once* for all," and that we are now free to move on into creative resurrection living.

The second consequence is that we fail to give adequate and serious attention to the real implications of the resurrection. We fail to appreciate the true enormity of what it is about. By limiting resurrection to being an "after death aspiration" we effectively turn it into a "non-event." Indeed, it could be said that we have allowed our understanding of resurrection to become *dependent upon and bound up with (our) death*, instead of seeing it an invitation to discover fresh vitality and resurrection aliveness in the present. As Girard notes: "resurrection is too real for a perception dimmed by the false transfigurations of mimetic idolatry" (Kirwan, *Discovering Girard*, 89). By this he means that by getting stuck in replaying the violence of the crucifixion, we fail to see what resurrection really means. This view is, of course, consistent with a church culture that is more interested in death than life.

Birthing Newness and Creativity

Resurrection is an on-going phenomenon. It reveals the real nature of humanity by allowing us to reconnect with the ever re-creative newness of God all around us, and so discover our vocation as co-creators with God. It is through striving to achieve this reconnection and embrace our vocation to creativity that we are encountered by, and caught up in, our destiny and inheritance: the fullness of the glory of God. As O'Leary remarks, "every baby is born to divinity" (1998, 132). Resurrection is the token of "full aliveness," the wholeness and shalom that God wishes us to experience.

Something of this vocation to be co-creators with God is glimpsed in Paul's letter to the Romans. He begins by reminding us that death has no more hold over us and that we are set free to live "according to the Spirit":

There is therefore now no condemnation for those who are in Christ Jesus. For the law of the Spirit of life in Christ Jesus has set you free from the law of sin and of death. For God has done what the law, weakened by the flesh, could not do: by sending his own Son in the likeness of sinful flesh, and to deal with sin, he condemned sin in the flesh, so that the just requirement of the law might be fulfilled in us, *who walk not according to the flesh but according to the Spirit.* For those who live according to the flesh set their minds on the things of the flesh, but those who live according to the Spirit set their minds on the things of the Spirit. To set the mind on the flesh is death, but to set the mind on the Spirit is life and peace (Rom 8:1-6, my emphasis).

The invitation to "walk not according to the flesh but according to the Spirit" is a call to let go of what binds us to the ways of death, and to live differently: to live the resurrection life. Paul characterizes this as being *adopted* by God and glorified with God as God's "children":

For you did not receive a spirit of slavery to fall back into fear, but you have received a spirit of adoption. When we cry, "Abba! Father!" it is that very Spirit bearing witness with our spirit that we are children of God, and if children, then heirs, heirs of God and joint heirs with Christ—if, in fact, we suffer with him *so that we may also be glorified with him* (8:15-17, my emphasis).

To be adopted by God and drawn into this process of "glorification" is to set out on a journey of discovery that God delights in us and gives us the highest of vocations. To join in the task of shaping our world and the various groups, communities, and nations of which we are a part, and of being shaped in response to the world in which we find ourselves, is to discover ourselves blessed and the object of God's pleasure. For "God saw everything that he had made, and indeed, it was very good" (Gen 1:31).

Absorbing the idea that *God delights in us*, and that aliveness and wholeness are real options for us, is no easy matter to accomplish. This is despite the fact that this is the message of the Easter—death *and* resurrection—event, and despite the fact that it is *only when we choose* to live this reality that the Spirit of creativity is given and we begin to live out our vocation to be co-creators with God!

Pentecost Moments

Luke's account in Acts of the outpouring of the Spirit describes Peter preaching to the crowds gathered in Jerusalem for Shavuot, the great commemoration of Moses and the Israelites receiving the Law on Mount Sinai. Both Shavuot and what we now call Pentecost are defining moments in the history of Jews and Christians. The story of "the rush of a violent wind, and … the [d]ivided tongues, as of fire, (2:2-3)" resting on each disciple, as well as the subsequent ability to be understood in the various languages present that day, have great resonance for all of us. So, too, the mass conversions and the way in which that early community shared "all things in common" (2:44).

However, in reality, this is but the story of the *first* Pentecost, and the account of what happened there is, inevitably, highly contextualized to that particular time and place. There is no reason to expect that, on every subsequent occasion that the Spirit has been poured out, the same specific things will have happened. For the ever-recreative Spirit of God responds differently according to people's needs, historical context, and frame of reference. For just as a close reading of the Gospels reveals how they each paint a different and evolving picture of Jesus—"as [a] 'messiah in process'" (Althaus-Reid, 2004, 48)—so, too, must our understanding of the Holy Spirit also be "in process," to enable us to discern its ever contemporary activity in the world.

What can be said for certain, though, is that the sign of the Spirit of God in action will always involve the galvanizing of individuals and the transformation of community *through an outpouring of creativity.*

Creativity Enters the World

When the Spirit is poured out at that first Pentecost, it removes forever the fear that, beginning with the women at the tomb (Mk 16:1-8), had confined the terrified disciples in an upper room (Jn 20). The Spirit liberates them from fear, and frees them to be creative in the world and to work with God to begin to reshape humanity into the image of Christ's own fullness. It frees us too, all these centuries later. Whenever the Spirit is given, people are *freed into their vocation to creativity.*

Yet as Nicolas Berdyaev points out, "there is not one word in the Gospel about creativeness" (*The Meaning of the Creative Act*, 2009, 96). And he goes on to surmise that "the Gospel's silence about creativeness is divinely wise … For the man who still lives wholly in the religious epoch of the law and the redemption is not conscious of his creative nature" (97).

According to Berdyaev the "epoch of the law" reveals human sinfulness, and the act of redemption in Christ restores freedom to humanity; but it is only with the coming of the Spirit that our real nature as co-creators with God is revealed. Berdyaev explains: "Creativeness is a work of man's God-like freedom, the revelation of the image of the Creator within him. Creativeness is not in the Father, neither is it in the Son but in the Spirit …. Where the Spirit is, there is freedom and there, too, is creativeness" (98). And, he adds: "In creativeness the divine in man is revealed by man's own free initiative, revealed from below rather than from above" (99).

This freedom to be creative does not mean that we can forget the death and resurrection of Jesus, or cease to celebrate it. But it does mean that, because of that single historic event, we are now empowered to embrace our true vocation as sons and daughters of God. We are fully liberated to become co-creators with God and able to explore our creativeness in the full confidence that this is what we are made for and what we *have been redeemed for.*

Sacramental Creativity

Not unexpectedly, however, the church has not lived up to this calling because it is still, despite its rhetoric, all too often trapped within a culture of death. It is caught up in an endless vicious circle of guilt and redemption, the two theological idols from which it cannot step away. As Berdyaev notes: "Love is new, creative life …" but, "[i]n the life of the Church love has been transformed into a dead and deadly word" (335). Is it now possible for the church to be freed into its own creativity?

As we have noted elsewhere, the Spirit of creativity cannot be confined to the church and is everywhere around us. And it may be, as Althaus-Reid (2007) suggests, that the recovery of the church lies in engagement with what she terms "secular inventiveness" (*Another Possible World,* edited by Althause-Reid, 2007, 167-177, *passim*). Secular inventiveness is a result of creative social action by individuals and groups that can take many forms. For instance, Althaus-Reid explores its relationship to the "goal of liberation" at the heart of liberation theology (167); its ability to critique religious, economic, or political ideologies wherever they are found; its capacity to create "historical projects" (171) for the flourishing of all people; and its facility for enabling "regime change" (174).

Such "inventiveness," rooted in secular thinking and practice, is nonetheless an expression of the Spirit of creativity at large in the world. It springs, not directly from religious or biblical origins—and is indeed often at complete variance with such beliefs—but may, even so, be considered to be the outworking of the process of incarnation in the world. More even than this, it is clear to Althaus-Reid, citing the liberation theologian Jon Sobrino, that the church has a great deal to learn from this expression of *secular* creativity:

> … if we must try to imagine what the gospel message would be if it were formulated today, it is becoming more and more obvious to Christians that secular inventiveness and creativity is more appropriate and fruitful (167).

This "secular inventiveness"—together with Mary Grey's "sacramental poetics" that seeks the transformation of everyday perception and experience (see Chapter Three)— forms the matrix for what might be termed the work of *sacramental creativity* that is now perhaps the real sacramentalism that the church is called to practice, perform, and proclaim.

Sacramental creativity places the discovery, naming, and celebration of creativity right at the heart of what it means to minister to, and among, individuals and communities. Encountering creative newness—welcoming it all around us, and giving ourselves permission to act and be co-creators with God—are at the heart of the transformation that our world needs. Our response to this God-given creative urge will shape the discipline, practice, and goals of a risk-shaped ministry that will both bless the world and reinvigorate the church.

Time to explore!

Here are some ideas for you to discuss with friends in your local church or community:

- Do you think the church expresses the right balance between the crucifixion and the resurrection?

- What is resurrection for you?

- Why are people afraid of newness?

Time for some action!

Here are some suggestions for you to try out:

- Take a walk around your neighborhood and community. Where are people experiencing crucifixion and resurrection?

- How is the church creative in your community? What could it learn from the secular world?

For church leaders:

- How does your ministry enable people to become co-creators with God and give birth to newness in the world?

- How might you begin to develop a public conversation about experiencing creativity, delight, and radical amazement, wherever it is found in your community?

- How might you enable your congregation to celebrate this in worship?

Part 2: Risk-Shaped Ministry

Being Faithful to the Future

Sacramental creativity—including the sacrament of naming and celebrating creativity in all its forms—is our recognition of, and response to, the God-given creative urge that the Spirit continues to pour out on all people.

The church is called to be at the forefront of the promotion and performance of this new sacramentality; not seeking to restrict which individuals and groups, or veto what kinds of creativity are to be included and celebrated, but rather delighting to engage with and share the task of blessing the human creative endeavor in all its forms and encouraging the fulfillment of our vocation to be co-creators with God. Such a sacramental ministry serves not only to acknowledge the diversity and value of human creativity itself, but also is a way to express a *faithful commitment to the future of humanity.* This is a task that cannot be limited to the church, but one that is entirely appropriate for the church to rank among its own urgent priorities, not least because the disciples of Jesus are called to be a community that ever looks to the future.

The story of Simeon and Anna (Lk 2:25-40) witnesses, in particular, to what it means to be faithful in recognizing and welcoming the future expression of the creative and transformative work of the Spirit.

Both Simeon and Anna long for the arrival of someone to open up the future for their nation. They do not know who it might be, though the Spirit had "revealed to [Simeon] … that he would not see death before he had seen the Lord's Messiah" (26). Despite the long years in the Temple—and the daily disappointment of waiting—they both remain ever receptive to the creative possibility of newness. They know in their bones that, with patience and imagination, they will be able to recognize and celebrate that future whenever it comes into the Temple. And, when it did arrive, *it is in the act of recognition and naming it* that this future becomes a present reality.

The particular discovery made that day was, of course, the infant Jesus, "destined" for the future transformation of the world. If the church today is to fulfill its own prophetic calling to serve this world with a refocused, re-energized, and re-creative sacramental ministry, then it must, like Simeon and Anna, play its role as a catalyst for change and newness. This will enable it to become a truly creative community through which the global human family is encouraged and empowered to imagine "life abundantly"—for all people—and to then turn that vision of fullness and flourishing into a tangible reality. But how might the church become such a community?

A Community of Adventure and Risk-Shaped Living

Not often since its earliest days has the church been a place for determined and courageous adventure and risk-taking. It has too frequently preferred to ally itself with the status quo and the powerful elites in our societies. It now needs to reconnect with its founding creative Spirit, and become once more a community that faithfully welcomes the future and embraces the risks and opportunities for service and ministry that flow from our experience of "adventuresome" discipleship, sacramental creativity, risk-shaped living, and of our calling to be co-creators with God.

From this experience of reconnection springs the desire to explore what expressions of risk-shaped living and creative adventure might look like, rooted—as they must be—within what Brock calls "a Christic community" (*Journeys by Heart*, 2008, *passim*). That is to say, it is rooted within a community that lives *authentically out of the recreative power* of the resurrection, one that seeks to embody creative, Christ-like action as the matrix for its ministerial practice.

This is not a straightforward vision to implement, however. For, notwithstanding the rhetoric on the church's belief in resurrection, all too often we fear the real implications of living out our faith in concrete ways; so we effectively collude together in restraining its demands on us and limiting its impact in the world. As Thomas Troeger observes: "Resurrection gives more freedom to Christ than most believers want their savior to have" (Troeger, *Preaching While the Church Is under Reconstruction*, 1999, 105). We can never quite comprehend the freedom the experience of resurrection gives to Christ, and that God is holding out to us. So we fail to grapple with the truly immense possibilities open to the creative and risk-shaped ministry that is our calling and our gift for the world.

The Marks of Risk-Shaped Ministry

A community of risk-shaped living values each moment, circumstance, and individual, and the potential they have for revealing the divine in our midst, for resurrection is ceaselessly at work, bringing new life out of deadness and offering manifold opportunities for our creative interaction with the divine. Risk-shaped living invites us "to risk the full calling of [our] creaturely life" (McIntosh, *Divine Teaching*, 180) in order to finally discover what it really means to be redeemed. And, once we have allowed ourselves to truly embrace our status as sons and daughters of God, risk-shaped living will embody and model a sacramental ministry that *requires* us to work as co-creators with God to forge our own meanings, values, and actions in the world, in the light of the Spirit's empowerment and creative blessing.

The effect of putting our "vocation to creativity" center-stage in the shaping of our ministry is quite dramatic. For it frees us to work to awaken each individual, moment, and situation to its God-given potential; and to release and enable transformation in the most creative and healing ways for every person, community, and age.

So what are the marks of risk-shaped ministry?

1. A Vocation to Proclaim Greater Personhood

The church needs to:

- embody the belief that everyone has a vocation to personhood, community, and service, and that the idea of vocation cannot be limited to certain authorized liturgical ministries

- champion the diversity of human personhood and seek to arouse the "Human Being" in everyone without exception

- become a more honest, open and intentionally therapeutic community that embraces new and essentially daring and risk-filled forms of loving service and ministry, and that empowers people to care for each other and for creation

- celebrate the myriad different expressions of what it means to live a spiritual life both by inviting people to explore the spiritual treasure houses of the Christian traditions and to seek a public dialogue about the spiritual nature and experience of life with those who do not attend

- enable people to more readily re-imagine their place in the world, reconnect with their true selves and with their neighbors, and so experience the universe to be full of enchantment, mystery, radical amazement, and breathtaking possibility

- free people and communities to express the human vocation to creativity

- work continuously with those outside its walls to help rescue God from the institutional and doctrinal imprisonment in which it routinely tends to bind God

2. A Desire to Become a Community of Fresh Revelation

The church needs to:

- reconnect with the subversive nature of Jesus' message, even at a cost to itself

- create liminal spaces of encounter and exchange for the celebration of our embodied experience of existence

- offer worship that is rooted in the desire to generate "the spiritual adventure of a lifetime," an opportunity for revaluing words, radical amazement, liberation into God's "shalom," experiencing the shock of the new, and reconnecting with the creative potential of each moment

- construct inclusive liturgies that are not founded on guilt, shame, or fear; but on the experience of the blessedness of all creation

- nourish people with "the edible bread of mysticism" by enabling them to be at ease in silence, darkness, and unknowing

- explore what worship and active discipleship offer for the sharing of a life-affirming discipleship

- seek to engage nonjudgmentally with the world and creation as part of the process of building up the kingdom-kindom of God

3. A Willingness to Speak a New Language

The church needs to:

- regain the simple vitality of Jesus' ministry and his facility for easy communication

- learn to listen hard without pronouncing judgments

- dare to be the guest of strangers and create a model of ministry that encourages conversations that open people to the possibility of mutual learning and transformation

- promote friendship as a mechanism for building good communities and developing relationships with those who are different

- turn fear, suspicion, and ambivalence, in all its forms, into opportunities for creative encounter

- develop a vocabulary for effectively exploring spiritual needs and experiences and a fluency in the language of desire that resonates with the experience of people as they explore their aspirations and need for fulfillment

- strive to promote wholeness and human flourishing by taking embodied experience seriously

4. A Mandate to Be an Economy of Blessing

The church needs to:

- develop a new model of pastoral care rooted in an affirmation of the blessedness of all creation, and encourage use of the imagination as a way to create not just new meanings but fresh possibilities for service and ministry

- engage with the sacramental creativity that is already happening by observing the rhythms, shapes, and contours taken by creativity in the secular world

- prioritize the need to "embed adventure" (see *The Faith of Leap*, Frost and Hirsch, 2011, 72), "foster a pioneer spirit" (145), and promote the spiritual practice of adventuresome living in the knowledge that the Spirit empowers us to be at the cutting edge of creative action and adventure, in partnership with the secular inventiveness already at work in our communities

- risk vulnerability and open-heartedness by facing down anxiety and fear in order to engage with what is strange, new, and perhaps still unformed

- accept the Spirit's invitation to find alternative ways of understanding leadership that promote the unconditional nurture, liberation, and flourishing of all people and communities; for in this lies true authority

- work to promote authenticity and transparency within its institutional life and structures

- say "yes" to the future (more than it colludes with the past) in order to become a creative part of an enlarged vision, and of the next stage of God's evolving relationship with humanity and with the world

Four Marks

These "four marks" of a risk-shaped ministry—and of the risk-taking Christian community they describe—are but new and contemporary interpretations of the traditional "four marks of the church" that seek to express its identity as "one, holy, catholic, and apostolic."

For the church's evolving struggle to understand "oneness"—initially as scattered "Bodies of Christ" holding diverse beliefs; as a single ecclesial, political, and doctrinal entity; at later times of denominational rivalry; or amid contemporary ideas about ecumenical "unity in diversity"— is historically more bound up with the desire for political power and allegiance, doctrinal authority, and the control of individual belief and behavior, than it is about the vocation to proclaim the greater personhood that is at the heart of Jesus' own ministry. Perhaps embracing *the oneness of our vocation to imitate Jesus* in striving for the real flourishing of all people— and placing this vocation above our preoccupation with ecclesiastical maneuvering, power games, and social status— would be a better, more worthy, and authentic manifestation of the presence of the Body of Christ in the world.

Similarly "holiness" is, arguably, more usefully sought in *the desire to be open* to *God* and focused on the "yet-more" of God's self-revelation in the world, and on becoming a community committed to discerning fresh revelation, valuing adventure and spiritual exploration, and seeking to live as ever more effective followers of Jesus for today's world, than in the urge to protect (the things of) God from contamination by worldliness, newness, strangeness, and otherness in all its forms. Perhaps the idea of holiness as "set-apart sacredness," purity, or moral and existential perfection has served as a disservice—to God and to us—both by ignoring or playing down the human experience of darkness, absence, and ambivalence in relation to God; as well as by its negative effect on our understanding of God and of our need to protect God from "the messiness" of the world.

Perhaps, too, "catholicity," in the sense of "that which is universally accepted and practiced," is more purposefully imagined in terms of the desire for *a shared experience of a global community of friendship and mutual hospitality*. This is one that welcomes difference and engages with diversity by seeking to understand and speak the common language of innate human desire, frustration, and longing. The idea that the sole hallmark of revelation, authenticity, and divine endorsement lies in the claim to universal beliefs, interpretations, and practices—and in the urge to *impose* these everywhere—rather than in the exploration, celebration, and basic trustworthiness of the commonality of human experience, flies in the face of Jesus' command for his disciples to encounter God's shalom—and our transformation—by being the guests of others and so build the community of difference that is the kingdom-kindom of God.

Finally, the idea of apostolicity raises important questions about the real nature and purpose of the church. The interpretation preferred by the religious hierarchies privileges the view that the church's authority resides in the teaching of the apostles passed down in an unbroken chain through the consecration of popes and bishops, or else as the supreme authority of the apostolic Scriptures themselves. This interrelationship between authority and teaching is manifested in the exercise of power and control over people's earthly lives and eternal destiny. In Matthew's gospel we hear Jesus say: "'All authority in heaven and on earth has been given to me. Go therefore and make disciples of all nations, baptizing them … and teaching them to obey everything that I have commanded you'" (Mt 28:18-20a). Meanwhile John links the giving of the Spirit to the apostles directly to their ministerial authority: "He said to them, 'Receive the Holy Spirit. If you forgive the sins of any, they are forgiven them; if you retain the sins of any, they are retained'" (Jn 20:22-23). As history has often shown, such authority can be too readily abused.

Perhaps a more helpful and life-giving interpretation of how the church might be truly apostolic can be caught from the vision of *the Body of Christ as an economy of blessing*. A "household" or "community" whose authority, ministry, and understanding of leadership lie in imitation of Jesus' living out of God's commandment to "be fruitful and multiply"; to be creative like God and a source of blessing for the world; and to say an unconditional "yes" to the future, whatever it holds.

The Calling of Those Who Minister

The call to risk-shaped ministry is not for the faint-hearted. It challenges many of the presuppositions of the Christian tradition, current theological thinking and ministerial formation that over-prioritize strategies for continuity with the past, conformity to sameness, and collusion with institutional modes of authority and models of leadership. There's nothing wrong per se with this approach; it is to be expected. But it won't change much in the world.

In contrast, those who seek to espouse a risk-shaped ministry will be able to appreciate both the challenges and the rewards of stepping outside the box of historic practice and outside "the parameters of decency" (Althaus-Reid, 2004, 7). They will identify the need to make church-going a thoroughly transformative experience that encourages and empowers people to move through *virtuous circles of change* in their self-understanding, theological and scriptural knowledge, practical discipleship, and commitment to responsible action in the wider community. Such risk-takers will have to face down the fear—of newness, difference, and otherness—in which most orthodox theology is rooted, in order to open up the creative theological responses demanded by the urgent need "to imagine life as it never was" (Althaus-Reid, *Another Possible World*, 2007, 7, quoting Fernando Pessoa), and then to turn that idea into a concrete experience of healing for our world.

Jesus' insistence that everyone should experience "fullness of life" or "have life abundantly" (Jn 10:10) is deeply problematic for our patriarchal religious institutions. It draws us beyond the limitations of our current theological discourse and worldview and puts us firmly on the growing edge of our discernment of God's ever fresh self-revelation. Risk-shaped ministry looks for the possibilities in the institutional and global crises that abound in our world. It seeks to respond to where God would have us be. And it points to the need to create a risk-shaped theology fit to empower human and planetary flourishing in the twenty-first century.

Time to explore!

Here are some ideas for you to discuss with friends in your local church or community:

- How do you understand Troeger's statement "resurrection gives more freedom to Christ than most believers want their savior to have"?

- What risks would you want your church to take?

- How, in your view, might the church be faithful to the future?

Time for some action!

Here are some suggestions for you to try out:

- Where is "adventure" happening in your community? In what practical ways can your church be a creative part of this?

- Where is risk-shaped ministry happening in your community? Who are the ministers? How might the church's ministry engage with this?

For church leaders:

- How does your ministry enable the church to take risks?

- In what ways do you think that orthodox theology might be "rooted in fear"?

Works Cited

Alison, James. *Faith beyond Resentment: Fragments Catholic and Gay.* London: Darton, Longman and Todd Ltd, 2001 (2006).

Althaus-Reid, Marcella. *From Feminist Theology to Indecent Theology: Readings on Poverty, Sexual Identity, and God.* London: SCM Press, 2004.

Althaus-Reid, Marcella Maria, Ivan Petrella, and Luiz Carlos Susin, ed. *Another Possible World.* London: SCM Press, 2007.

Back, Les. *The Art of Listening.* Oxford: Berg, 2007.

Basset, Lytta. *Holy Anger: Jacob, Job, Jesus.* London: Continuum, 2007.

Beck, Ulrich. *A God of One's Own: Religion's Capacity for Peace and Potential for Violence.* Translated by Rodney Livingstone. Cambridge: Polity Press, 2010.

Berdyaev, Nicolas. *The Meaning of the Creative Act.* San Rafael, CA: Semantron Press, 2009.

Berry, Thomas. *The Sacred Universe: Earth, Spirituality, and Religion in the Twenty-First Century.* Mary Evelyn Tucker, ed. New York: Columbia University Press, 2009.

Bhabha, Homi K. *The Location of Culture.* London: Routledge, 1994.

Biddington, Terry. *Risk-Shaped Discipleship: On Going Deeper into the Life of God.* San José, CA: Resource Publications, Incorporated, 2010.

__________. "Spirituality in the Market-place." *The Way* 46/4 (October 2007): 113-126. Oxford: Society of Jesus.

Brock, Rita Nakashima. *Journeys by Heart: A Christology of Erotic Power.* Eugene, OR: Wipf and Stock, 2008.

Brueggemann, Walter. *Mandate to Difference. An Invitation to the Contemporary Church.* Louisville: Westminster John Knox Press, 2007.

__________. *The Message of the Psalms: A Theological Commentary.* Minneapolis: Augsburg Publishing House, 1984.

__________. *Redescribing Reality: What We Do When We Read the Bible.* London: SCM Press, 2009.

__________. *The Threat of Life: Sermons on Pain, Power, and Weakness.* Foreword by Charles Campbell. Minneapolis: Augsburg Press, 1996.

__________. *The Word Militant: Preaching a Decentering Word.* Minneapolis: Fortress Press, 2007.

Clarkson, Petruska. *Gestalt Counselling in Action.* 2nd Edition. London: SAGE Publications, Ltd, 1999.

Cupitt, Don. *Above Us Only Sky: The Religion of Ordinary Life.* Santa Rosa, CA: Polebridge Press, 2008.

De La Torre, Miguel. *A Lily Among the Thorns: Imagining a New Christian Sexuality.* San Francisco: Jossey-Bass, 2007.

Douglas-Klotz, Neil. *The Hidden Gospel: Decoding the Spiritual Message of the Aramaic Jesus.* Wheaton, IL: Quest Books, 1999.

Edgar, Iain R. *Guide to Imagework: Imagination-Based Research Methods.* London: Routledge, 2004.

Fanthorpe U. A. "Friends' Meeting House, Frenchay, Bristol." *New and Collected Poems.* Enitharmon Press, 2010. Quoted here by permission of Dr. R. V. Bailey.

Fiddes, Paul S. *Participating in God: A Pastoral Doctrine of the Trinity.* London: Darton, Longman and Todd, 2000.

Firet, Jacob. *Dynamics in Pastoring.* Grand Rapids, MI: Wm. B. Eerdmans Publishing Company, 1986.

Frost, Michael and Alan Hirsch. *The Faith of Leap: Embracing a Theology of Risk, Adventure & Courage.* Grand Rapids, MI: Baker Books, 2011.

Grey, Mary C. *Sacred Longings: Ecofeminist Theology and Globalization.* London: SCM Press, 2003.

Gubi, Peter Madsen. *Prayer in Counselling and Psychotherapy: Exploring a Hidden Meaningful Dimension.* London: Jessica Kingsley Publishers, 2008.

Hauerwas, Stanley. *Performing the Faith: Bonhoeffer and the Practice of Nonviolence.* London: Society for Promoting Christian Knowledge, 2004.

Hodge, Daniel White. "No Church in the Wild: Hip Hop Theology and Mission" in *Missiology: An International Review* 41, no. 1 (Jan. 2013):97-109. London: SAGE.

Kirwan, SJ, Michael. *Discovering Girard.* London: Darton, Longman and Todd Ltd, 2004.

Knust, Jennifer Wright. *Unprotected Texts: The Bible's Surprising Contradictions About Sex and Desire.* New York: HarperOne, 2011.

Larkin, Philip. *Collected Poems.* London: Faber and Faber Limited, 2003.

McFadyen, A. *The Call to Personhood: A Christian Theory of the Individual in Social Relationships.* Cambridge: Cambridge University Press, 1990.

McFague, Sallie. *Speaking in Parables: A Study in Metaphor and Theology.* London: SCM Press, 1975.

McIntosh, Mark A. *Divine Teaching: An Introduction to Christian Theology.* Oxford: Blackwell Publishing, 2008.

Morisy, Ann. *Bothered and Bewildered: Enacting Hope in Troubled Times.* London: Continuum International Publishing Group, 2009.

Morton, Cole. "A New Dawn. How Britain became a Pagan Nation." *The Guardian*, 22.06.09. www.guardian. co.uk/world/2009/jun/22/paganism-stonehenge-environmentalism-witchcraft.

O'Leary, Daniel, J. *Lost Soul?: The Catholic Church Today.* Blackrock: Columba Press, 1999.

__________. *Passion for the Possible: A Spirituality of Hope for a New Millennium.* Blackrock: Columba Press, 1998.

Pfeiffer, Franz. *Meister Eckhart.* Translated by C. de B. Evans. London: John M Watkins, 1956.

Primavesi, Anne. *Sacred Gaia: Holistic Theology and Earth System Science.* London: Routledge, 2000.

Randriamampionona, A. *"Difference as Ferment for the Hybrid Church."* Ph.D. thesis, Manchester University, 2012.

Ruusbroec, John. *The Spiritual Espousals and Other Works.* Translated by James A. Wiseman, O.S.B. New York: Paulist Press, 1985.

Sandercock, Leonie. *Cosmopolis II: Mongrel Cities in the 21st Century.* London: Continuum, 2003.

Shannahan, Chris. "'NEET' believers? An analysis of 'belief' on an urban housing estate." *Culture and Religion: An Interdisciplinary Journal* 13:3, 315-335. London: Routledge, 2012.

Shea, John. *Gospel Light: Jesus Stories for Spiritual Consciousness.* New York: Crossroad Publishing Company, 1998.

Soelle, Dorothee. *The Silent Cry: Mysticism and Resistance.* Translated by Barbara and Martin Runscheidt. Minneapolis: Augsburg Fortress Press, 2001.

Swinton, John. *Resurrecting the Person: Friendship and the Care of People with Mental Health Problems.* Nashville: Abingdon Press, 2000.

Troeger, Thomas H. *Preaching While the Church Is under Reconstruction: The Visionary Role of Preachers in a Fragmented World.* Nashville: Abingdon Press, 1999.

Ward, Pete. *Participation and Mediation: A Practical Theology for the Liquid Church.* London: SCM Press, 2008.

Watts, Alan W. *The Wisdom of Insecurity: A Message for an Age of Anxiety.* London: Rider & Co, 1976.

Weber, Hans Rudi. Cited on the website of the Diocese of Bath and Wells, UK:http://www.bathandwells.org.uk/formation/why-have-a-school-of-formation. Accessed June 17, 2013.

Willows, David and John Swinton, ed. *Spiritual Dimensions of Pastoral Care: Practical Theology in a Multidisciplinary Context.* London: Jessica Kingsley Publishers, 2000.

Wilson, Michael. "Personal Care and Political Action." 1985. *Spiritual Dimensions of Pastoral Care: Practical Theology in a Multidisciplinary Context.* 170-178. London: Jessica Kingsley Publishers, 2000.

Wink, Walter. *The Human Being: Jesus and the Enigma of the Son of Man.* Minneapolis: Augsburg Fortress Press, 2002.

Wright, Alex. *Why Bother with Theology?* London: Darton, Longman and Todd Ltd, 2002.